MYTHBUSTING
THE GREAT
OUTDOORS

MYTHBUSTING THE GREAT OUTDOORS

What's True and What's Not?

JAMIE SIEBRASE

Illustrations by Olivia Wischmeyer

ESSEX, CONNECTICUT

FALCON®

An imprint of Globe Pequot, the trade division of The Rowman &
  Littlefield Publishing Group, Inc.
4501 Forbes Blvd., Ste. 200
Lanham, MD 20706
www.rowman.com

Falcon and FalconGuides are registered trademarks and Make Adventure
  Your Story is a trademark of The Rowman & Littlefield Publishing
  Group, Inc.
Distributed by NATIONAL BOOK NETWORK

British Library Cataloguing in Publication Information available

Library of Congress Cataloging-in-Publication Data
Names: Siebrase, Jamie, author.
Title: Mythbusting the great outdoors : what's true and what's not /
  Jamie Siebrase ; illustrations by Olivia Wischmeyer.
Description: Guilford, Connecticut : Falcon Guides, 2022.
Identifiers: LCCN 2022017691 (print) | LCCN 2022017692 (ebook) |
  ISBN 9781493063475 (paperback) | ISBN 9781493063482 (epub)
Subjects: LCSH: Outdoor life. | Wilderness survival.
Classification: LCC GV191.6 .S54 2022 (print) | LCC GV191.6 (ebook) |
  DDC 796.5—dc23/eng/20220603
LC record available at https://lccn.loc.gov/2022017691
LC ebook record available at https://lccn.loc.gov/2022017692

♾™ The paper used in this publication meets the minimum requirements
of American National Standard for Information Sciences—Permanence of
Paper for Printed Library Materials, ANSI/NISO Z39.48-1992.

For Ben

Contents

Acknowledgments

I couldn't do anything without my husband, Ben, and his ongoing support and love.

Thanks to my editor, Katie O'Dell, for providing the fodder and fuel for this book, and to my dad for being my unofficial editor and first reader. I'm lucky to have in-laws who know a lot about the great outdoors: A special thank you to Jon for providing feedback on my wolf chapter, and to Susanne and Ron for reviewing the chapters on mushrooms and moss.

I really appreciate Kathy and Gary Webster. Even though they barely knew me, my new neighbors were willing to read several of the chapters in this book and answer pretty much any science-related question I threw their way. My Aunt Barbara (a chemist) has also been an invaluable fact-checking resource.

I'd like to acknowledge fellow Falcon authors Rob Coppolillo and Nathan Summers for offering their expertise and for reviewing my chapters on avalanches and fire, respectively. All the sources cited in this book provided crucial information, but a few people went above and beyond what I expected. A special thanks to wolf biologist David Mech, mycologist Michael Beug, bryologist Janice Glime, Greg Schoor from the National Weather Service, Leave No Trace's Ben Lawhon, Professor Lindy Rossow, and Erik Kulick, who owns and operates the True North Wilderness Survival School.

Introduction

You only ever grow as a human being if you're outside your comfort zone.
—Scott Jurek, who ran the Appalachian Trail in 46 days, 8 hours, and 7 minutes in 2015

This book took me way outside of my comfort zone. Outdoors enthusiasts love to talk about "Type II Fun." You know, hiking up a tall mountain, straight into the wind, and then eating pinto beans from the can before sleeping on a bed of cold rocks.

Type II Fun can be anything that's miserable in the moment, but fun to remember once you're warm and have regained access to a flush toilet (see "Everything You Never Wanted to Know about Pooping Outdoors"). Writing this book was Type II Fun. While it was incredibly engaging to spend my days interviewing a variety of scientists, doctors, and professors about subjects ranging from celestial navigation to sharks, this whole project has given me terrible insomnia. I'll wake up at 3:00 a.m. in a sheer panic, thinking about the myths in the pages that follow, wondering what novel discovery will turn my hard-won fact-finding into a brand new misconception.

As astronomer Carl Sagan put it, "Science is not perfect." In fact, he has described science as "self-correcting" and "ever-changing." The *Merriam-Webster* dictionary defines science as "knowledge about or study of the natural world based on facts learned through experiments and observation." That last bit is especially important. Scientists continually perform new experiments that lead to fresh observations. But scientists don't simply add additional facts to a vast domain of existing knowledge: Rather, they question prior conclusions as new evidence rolls in. As such, accepted truths are always subject to change.

That's my disclaimer. I tried my best to incorporate into this book the most up-to-date facts available. Some facts could conceivably evolve over time, but hopefully by then I'll be dead or so old nobody will expect me to rewrite this book.

I wrote this book because my editor, Katie, didn't like any of the other ideas I'd sent her, and so out of sympathy she pitched a concept to me. I have degrees in writing and law; I wasn't a scientist when I started writing this book. And yet, when I could get my sources to slow down and explain things to me in simple, everyday language, I found all the technical subject matter fascinating and surprisingly accessible.

This project took off last winter, when it was really cold and dark outside. Usually I get a little depressed in January and February, but against all odds, 2021 was different. My kids were home 24/7 during the pandemic. They were always in my hair, probably because I was homeschooling them, administering a project-based curriculum I'd ordered online. Our favorite part of the day was usually science. Science projects, specifically, and we were spending an unprecedented amount of time outdoors in nature.

My kids' curiosity about the natural world was contagious, and at the same time, I was conducting interviews with experts on some really strange things such as moss sex and wiping your butt with pinecones. My wonder with my surroundings grew suddenly—exponentially—like a colony of bacteria. Something shifted. I started seeing everything around me differently.

Maybe it was a form of escapism, a way to get away from my family on a couple of Saturdays a month, but in the spring, I enrolled in an herbalism certificate program at the Denver

Botanic Gardens. I was having so much fun going on plant identification hikes and becoming an amateur botanist that one morning, before I'd had enough coffee, I signed up for a 14-month-long Community Naturalist program through the Denver Audubon Society. I couldn't confidently spell Audubon at the time, but I've since become a pseudo-expert on an array of subjects, from local geology and meteorology to Colorado birds, bugs, fish, and mammals. I still don't have a formal degree in anything scientific, but I proudly consider myself a community scientist.

All this to say that *Mythbusting the Great Outdoors* ignited within me a passion I never knew existed. I hope this book sparks a childish sense of wonder in you, too, and that you don't give me too much guff if any of the facts in the following pages change over time.

The Truth about Avalanches

Yodelayhee—shhh! You're shredding through Colorado's pristine backcountry on a crisp February morning, warm to the toes thanks to your wool socks, and everybody in your group is doing their part to keep it down because just one shrill scream could set off a deadly avalanche. Right?

Only if you're skiing across a movie. The sound-triggering myth is a Hollywood legend, according to Ethan Greene, PhD, the director of the Colorado Avalanche Information Center, a Colorado Department of Natural Resources program providing avalanche information and education.

A handful of modern films reference sound as an avalanche trigger. Take the classic 1969 spy film, *On Her Majesty's Secret Service*, for example, the sixth in the James Bond series. Endless blue skies stretch out over the snow-capped Bernese Alps, but beyond the peaceful heavens it's mostly mayhem on camera as George Lazenby and Diana Rigg attempt to dodge a super-villain and her henchmen by skiing out of the secluded Swiss village of Lauterbrunnen.

During a nerve-racking chase scene, the duo skis right past a large yellow sign with a massive red *X*. The action halts for several beats, and the cameraman homes in on the writing. "Ruhe! Quiet! Silence!" it reads, warning: "Avalanche area." Jimmy Stewart perpetuates the sound-triggering myth in *The Mountain Road*, a 1960s war film with a well-known avalanche scene. And as recently as 2013, Mickey Mouse carried on the falsehood while shushing a yeti during the Disney short *Yodelberg*.

The silver screen isn't the only source disseminating misinformation. Sound—that is, shouting, a sharp noise—is mentioned as a potential avalanche trigger in several books, too, according to Swiss researchers Benjamin Reuter and Jürg Schweizer, who studied the sound-triggering myth and presented their findings in 2009 at the International Snow Science Workshop in Davos, Switzerland.

Spoiler alert: It's definitely a myth that noise triggers avalanches.

An avalanche is a sudden, massive fall of snow, ice, and rocks down a slope. Simply put, force causes avalanches. Sometimes that force is gravity, but external forces like the weight of a skier or fresh falling snow can also trigger avalanches. Sound waves are a force capable of moving things (think: bumping speakers) . . . but they aren't powerful enough to move snow down a mountainside.

During World War I, over 60,000 soldiers died in avalanches while fighting in the Alps, making the terrifying slides more deadly to Italian and Austrian troops than poisonous gas. The sound-trigger myth didn't emerge in force, though, until the 1940s, when World War II soldiers reported setting off avalanches with their artillery. Apparently American soldiers just assumed it was the sound of their weapons that triggered spontaneous torrents of snow.

This history surrounding the origins of the sound-triggering myth might give off the impression that terrified young men fighting far from home were ambushed by an unknown landscape. But actually, Americans knew about avalanches, at least to some degree, before the world wars commenced. "Our deadliest avalanche in history occurred in 1910," says Rob Coppolillo, International Federation of Mountain Guides Association certified guide and Falcon author.

The Wellington Avalanche of March 1, 1910, overtook railroad passengers traveling across Stevens Pass, a mountain pass through the Cascades in Washington. During a routine winter trip from Seattle to Spokane, a 14-foot-high wall of snow slammed into two train cars that had been stuck in drifts of snow for days. The avalanche swept Pullmans filled with passengers into the Tye River gorge, killing 96 men, women, and children.

The disaster put railroad tycoons on high alert, yet during the war years, Coppolillo explains, "Avalanches were less a recreational hazard and more one associated with mining, roads, and infrastructure." It's possible then that many American soldiers fighting in WWII had heard about avalanches back home but only witnessed them for the first time overseas.

GIs might have misinterpreted the situation when they (falsely) "observed" the sound of their gunfire triggering avalanches. Their ignorance, though, paved the way for present-day avalanche safety measures. The Military Artillery for Avalanche Control Program, for one, uses artillery and explosives to control avalanches through preplanned triggering. And this is one thing that really confuses a lot of people. Explosives make a very loud noise and then—voilà—an avalanche barrels down a mountainside like a terrifying tsunami of snow.

But there is more to dynamite than just sound. There's the explosion itself, of course, and it's actually dynamite's "explosive force" that incites the avalanche, says Coppolillo. He elaborates, "To trigger an avalanche, you need to introduce some new load or force to the snowpack, so much that it pushes the snowpack past its 'breaking point.'"

The weight of a skier can—and often does—push snow-pack to its limits. What about sound, though, versus the direct pressure of body weight? That's exactly what Reuter and Schweizer tested in their study.

Sound produces pressure waves in air. All waves will dissipate over distance and completely change when they interact with solids, such as frozen water (snow) or land. Sound waves, in fact, decrease in intensity while traveling through the air and then are absorbed on impact when they hit snow or earth.

It's important to understand that shock waves and sound waves are two totally different things. "Shock waves might be responsible for the crash of thunder, the boom of fireworks, the bang of a gunshot, and the blast from a nuclear explosion . . . but they aren't just really big noises," explains professor of mechanical engineering Gary S. Settles, PhD, writing for *American Scientist*. Sound waves, Settles writes, are kind of like the weaker cousins of shock waves.

In their sound-triggering study, Reuter and Schweizer looked at all sorts of waves, including the sound waves created from a person shouting at the bottom of a slope, the acoustic pressure waves from approaching helicopters and aircrafts, and shock waves caused by detonations. They even examined the pressure a skier's static weight placed on snowpack.

Reuter and Schweizer pored over their data and drew up equations, all to determine that a loud human scream, with its pressure amplitude of 2 pascals, doesn't have nearly enough oomph to set off an avalanche. It takes something highly energetic to trigger an avalanche. Parents may disagree, but a shrill toddler scream isn't energetic by scientific standards!

Reuter and Schweizer claim it takes between 200 and 500 pascals of pressure to prematurely trigger an avalanche. So even a jet plane, at 20 pascals, won't usually cut it. In fact, a supersonic boom (200 pascals) barely does the trick. When ski resorts and mountain monitoring groups trigger avalanches for preventative safety, they use explosives generating between 1,000 and 1,500 pascals of pressure.

That is just one study, of course. Nobody knows exactly how much pressure is needed to trigger an avalanche, and there is a slew of variables to consider. Avalanches, for example, are heavily dependent on existing conditions, and experts will talk about a "tipping point" when they're trying to get non-geoscientists to understand that certain environments are especially conducive to avalanching.

As snow piles up in avalanche terrain, the chances of an avalanche occurring become more and more likely until, eventually, they'll happen on their own. And so while it takes pressure to prematurely trigger an avalanche, thanks to the force of gravity, the amount of pressure needed decreases as an avalanche becomes closer to spontaneously occurring. Picture a bell curve, not a straight line, when you're thinking about this temporal progression.

All things considered, though, it is unlikely—like, really, really, highly unlikely—that a human voice could ever cause an avalanche, even when one's about to occur naturally.

"We don't have any documented cases of sound triggering avalanches," Greene says. And as Reuter and Schweizer note in their report, "At times of high instability, when natural avalanches are frequently observed, a coincidence of shouting and releasing may occur, but it will not be possible to claim that the release had been caused by the shouting."

Reuter and Schweizer conclude, "It can be ruled out that shouting or loud noise can trigger snow slab avalanches . . . Triggering by sound really is a myth."

But wait, the careful reader noticed that Reuter and Schweizer looked specifically at slab avalanches. And, yes, just in case you thought you had it figured out, there are actually several types of avalanches to consider.

Two sets of snow conditions (slab/loose, dry/wet) intersect to create four types of avalanches: dry slab, wet slab, dry loose, and wet loose. "Over the course of a season, most locations

with a seasonal snowpack will encounter all of these avalanches," explains Coppolillo. But slab avalanches are the most
lethal, accounting for nearly every avalanche death in North
America.

In cold, mountainous areas, there are many layers of snow
that form the snowpack Coppolillo references. It's easy to
picture how this works: At the beginning of the snow season, a
fresh dusting covers the bare ground; then it snows again, and
that next snowfall covers the first layer, and so on and so forth.

Slab avalanches start with a layer of cohesive snow—a
slab—resting on top of another slab. If the deeper, buried layer
is weak, well, it doesn't take much force—maybe just the weight
of one skier—to shatter the lower slab like a pane of glass.

When the slab breaks off from the rest of the snowpack,
it comes tumbling down. We're talking about tons, if not
thousands of tons, of material. And remember, Greene says,
"Snowpack that collects on the mountains is solid material."
Greene describes the consistency as cement. It's nothing like
the light fluffy stuff that falls in your front yard.

Loose snow avalanches, on the other hand, are exactly
what they sound like: Snow that's loose—that is, not part of
a cohesive slab—sliding down a mountainside. "It's like sugar
perched on a slope . . . or loose sand," Coppolillo says.

Experts identify loose snow avalanches by their fan-
like shape. In fact, sometimes they're called "point-release
avalanches" because the slide starts at a very specific point
and then accumulates material while moving downhill. The
smallest loose snow avalanches are referred to as sluffs, and
while they're usually harmless to people, they can cause major
property damage. And there's always the possibility that a sluff
will trigger a deadlier slab avalanche.

Avalanche experts differentiate between dry and wet
avalanches, too, because, well, they're two distinct things. Wet
avalanches are more common in the North Cascades and the
Sierra Nevada, and they tend to occur in the spring, though

Coppolillo notes that "seasonal avalanche patterns have certainly shifted due to climate change."

There's also a wet-dry continuum to consider. Some avalanches are best described as "moist," and it's not uncommon for avalanches to start out dry and then end up wet by the time they reach the bottom of a mountain. "This is a function of different snow becoming involved in the avalanche as it travels downslope," Coppolillo says, explaining that snow doesn't change from dry to moist as it moves downhill. Instead, he adds that dry snow from higher-up avalanches entrains wet snow at lower elevations.

For our purposes, though, these distinctions really don't matter. "I don't know of any research that has looked at the sound-triggering myth in relation to different types of avalanches," Greene says. There hasn't been that much effort or funding put into this sector of avalanche research. And that's simply because experts haven't observed that sounds trigger avalanches.

Big snow, wind, and precipitation storms cause spontaneous slab avalanches while rapid warming events set off wet avalanches. Humans trigger avalanches prematurely with their weight while skiing, snowboarding, snowshoeing, and snowmobiling through avalanche terrain.

Some outdoors enthusiasts mistakenly think avalanches occur only in the winter months.

Historically and annually, more people die in avalanches in Colorado than anywhere else in the country. While they're most common from November to April, avalanches can—and do—happen every month of the year in Colorado, even mid-August.

That has as much to do with the snow as the people who visit. Colorado is a popular vacation destination providing access to many high-mountain areas conducive to avalanching.

Six people die a year in Colorado, on average, from avalanches (compared to an average of 27 avalanche deaths per year across the United States).

It's amazing that number's so low, really, considering that during a typical avalanche season, Colorado usually records somewhere around 4,000 to 5,000 avalanches. "That's estimated to be only about 10 percent, maybe less, maybe only 1 percent, of the avalanches that actually occur," Greene explains, pointing out that most avalanches will go completely undetected.

In snow and windstorms, it's crazy-hard to see high alpine peaks. So a lot of avalanches that run during storms will then get covered up by subsequent snowstorms. "There are literally thousands and thousands of avalanches every winter through-out the western US," adds Coppolillo.

In about 90 percent of human-avalanche incidents, the victim (or somebody in their party) triggered the slide. If you're going to be out recreating in avalanche terrain, you've got to know how to avoid triggering avalanches.

Since sound doesn't trigger avalanches, walking quietly through the woods isn't a good avoidance strategy. And please don't plan on diving out of the way.

It's a common misconception that humans can outski or outrun avalanches.

Avalanches move fast, up to 80 miles per hour, according to the Utah Avalanche Center, so you aren't going to outrun or outski one. Even a snowmobile can't move that fast. Taking shelter behind a big object like a tree will probably not help much either, since an avalanche slides with tremendous force.

There are, however, several useful strategies for outdoors enthusiasts to employ. First and foremost, Greene says, "Check the avalanche forecast before you go out." That is, hands down, the most important safety practice anyone can follow.

Most urban areas, including Denver, Salt Lake, Seattle, and Reno, have reliable forecast centers that give users great advice on days to avoid the mountains altogether, as well as safer days to go out. For current information, check out the website https://avalanche.org.

It's also important to take an avalanche safety class. Short, online courses are probably sufficient for people who plan to avoid avalanche terrain while recreating. Through its website, the Colorado Avalanche Information Center offers a 15-minute educational video that teaches participants how to recognize treacherous avalanche zones, which is actually pretty simple since avalanches occur on very specific inclines.

Angle matters, and for an avalanche to get going, a slope must be between 30 and 55 degrees in steepness. Snow sheds on slopes that are any steeper, meaning it just sort of runs downhill before it's able to build up enough to be dangerous. Snow on shallow slopes doesn't usually slip at all.

Some winter athletes can't be confined to avalanche-free areas. If you'll be shredding through diverse terrain, you really need to take a field course, one where you go out with an instructor. During proper field courses, participants learn to recognize obvious signs of instability, such as cracking in the snow and so-called whumpf sounds—both are strong indicators that the avalanche process is under way.

Carrying the right equipment is also essential when recreating in avalanche terrain. Everyone in your group needs an avalanche rescue transceiver (i.e., a personal location beacon), a probe pole, and a shovel.

"You won't have time for an outside rescue if you get buried," Coppolillo explains. You'll be counting on your friends to dig you out.

It's really hard—almost impossible—to find people who are buried in snow unless they're wearing a transceiver. Assuming your friends find you, preferably in 15 minutes or less, they're going to use their shovels to free you from the heavy snowpack.

Here's another myth to dispel: A lot of people are under the false impression that if you're buried in an avalanche, you should spit so you'll know which way is up.

There's even an old 1987 episode of *MacGyver* ("Out in the Cold") in which Richard Dean Anderson narrowly escapes demise using this exact tactic. The idea is that if you know which direction is up, then you can simply dig your way out.

That's not a viable emergency backup plan. If you're encased in snow, it's not like you're in a snow cave, just hanging out. You're buried in a substance that's so dense some victims can't even expand their lungs enough to breathe. You can't throw things, you can't spit, and even if you're buried with your head sticking up, you'll probably still need someone else to dig you out.

Remember, Coppolillo adds, "It's rare that people get killed by random avalanches." Usually our weight triggers the slides that kill us, and of course that means we can avoid triggering them, too. In most cases there are plenty of warning signs that snowpack is unstable and has the potential to slide. To minimize your risk, learn to identify avalanche-prone slopes, and then choose safer routes to travel.

BOTTOM LINE: We can stop shushing each other during winter adventures. Despite ample evidence to the contrary, it remains a popular belief that human voices cause premature avalanches. There's plenty to worry about when it comes to avalanches, and every reason to be prepared, but a chatty companion or a screaming child isn't something worth stressing over.

What's the North Star Good for Anyway?

"Celestial navigation has been used, and used very accurately, for hundreds of years," begins Captain Cynthia Robson, a master mariner and instructor of celestial navigation at the Merchant Marine Academy in Kings Point, New York.

Back in the 1980s, when the hairstyles were bolder and GPS wasn't fully operational yet, sailors like Robson had a number of options for electronic navigation, including Decca, Omega, Transit, and Doppler. And yet none of these systems were as exciting to Robson as using a special navigation tool (a sextant) to measure the angles of celestial bodies in order to determine her latitude and longitude. "It's a rush when you work out a long calculation and get it right," Robson says.

The US Naval Academy made headlines in 2006 when it terminated its celestial navigation curriculum. But by 2015, Annapolis was once again teaching enlisted ranks how to cross the high seas by star. The Merchant Marine Academy in Kings Point, on the other hand, has continuously taught celestial navigation.

As GPS became more reliable in the 1990s, and internationally available, Robson continues, "Other types of navigation systems were basically shut down." So in one sense, celestial navigation is more important than ever . . . because if GPS fails, navigators no longer have access to an alternative means of fixing their position.

Basically, celestial navigators use a watch plus a sextant to calculate their position on a nautical chart. The process requires a reference point. Midday, the sun is a great point of reference, but at night, Polaris is a popular target. Using a sextant to navigate is complicated, and a tutorial is way beyond the scope of this book. For those who are really interested in learning more, there are introductory videos available on YouTube.

Finding Polaris

If you're planning to navigate with Polaris, first you'll have to find it. Wait until it's dark. Put on a coat if you'd like (see "Here's How Cold Weather Really Impacts Human Health"). Then walk outside. Are you in the Northern Hemisphere, above the Tropic of Cancer, in the mid-latitude or high-latitude regions? Excellent, because the North Star is only visible north of the equator, and it's only visible every single night if you're at least 30 degrees north of the equator. (That translates to anywhere in North America, for easy reference.)

From here, look up, and locate the Big Dipper, a prominent pattern in the constellation Ursa Major, with seven stars forming a handle with a bowl. There are two twinkling orbs on the side of the Big Dipper's bowl, opposite the handle. These stars, Merak and Dubhe, lead to Polaris.

Starting from Merak, fixed at the bottom of the bowl, draw a line toward Dubhe, on the bowl's lip. But don't stop at Dubhe. Take your imaginary line, and extend it roughly five times to reach a star that's similar in brightness. Voilà! Perched about 430 light-years away—just over 2,500 trillion miles above Earth—there's Polaris, the North Star, a.k.a. Pole Star or Alpha Ursae Minoris.

Technically the Little Dipper will also lead you to Polaris since the North Star marks the end of its handle. But the Little Dipper is tougher to spot.

You really won't need a pitch-black night in an International Dark Sky Park to see Polaris. The darker the airspace, the better, though, because contrary to popular belief, the North Star is only about the 50th brightest star in the night sky.

It's a common and enduring misconception that the North Star is the brightest star in the night sky.

"Maybe it's 49, maybe it's 51, depending on what other stars are doing," says astronomer Rick Fienberg, PhD, former press officer for the American Astronomical Society, a community of professional astronomers headquartered in Washington, DC.

Star brightness waxes and wanes, and the North Star itself is a "variable star," Fienberg explains, with fluctuating levels of brilliance. But Polaris's variances are so subtle, you'd be hard-pressed to notice them with the naked eye.

While it's not the brightest, Polaris certainly stands out. Even in a light-polluted city, even when a full moon's sheen hides other orbs, the North Star is still relatively easy to spot. Scientists have measured star brightness in magnitudes ever since 129 BCE, when the ancient Greek astronomer Hipparchus described the radiance of stars on a 1 to 6 magnitude scale.

The lower the magnitude, the brighter the star glows. Each change in magnitude is "about 2.512-something-or-other times fainter or brighter, depending on what way you're going," Fienberg says. A magnitude 1 star, then, is about 100 times brighter than a magnitude 6 star. And since Hipparchus's time, astronomers have realized that some stars are actually brighter than magnitude 1. Take, for example, Sirius, the "Dog Star" of the Canis Major constellation. At magnitude −1.46—that's *negative* 1.46, emphasis on the minus sign—it's the brightest nighttime star in our sky.

The faintest stars we can see with the naked eye are typically magnitude 6, though in, say, the middle of rural New Mexico, the human eye might be able to detect a magnitude 7 or 7.5 shimmer. A good backyard telescope gets an amateur astronomer down to magnitude 16 or 17, but to see our galaxy's really faint stars, you'll need the Hubble Space Telescope, which can detect stars as faint as magnitude 25.

"Polaris is a second magnitude star," Fienberg says, adding, "That's not too shabby." And if you didn't know much about the night sky, it would actually be pretty reasonable to assume that Polaris is the brightest night star. A lot of people are under this (mistaken) impression.

When asked why so many people believe the North Star is the brightest star, Fienberg theorizes that, "People know there's something special about Polaris because it has a special name." Brightness, however, isn't what makes the North Star special.

You know that annoying adage realtors are always spouting off? With the North Star, it's all about location, location, location! "Polaris doesn't sit directly on Earth's North Celestial Pole, but it's pretty dang close," Fienberg says, explaining that "Polaris's position lines up, almost perfectly, with Earth's axis." And that's the North Star's real claim to fame.

The North Celestial Pole is an extension of the Earth's geographic North Pole. If you extend Earth's rotation axis straight up into the sky, it'd be very close to Polaris. "Polaris is offset just a bit—less than a degree—from the North Celestial Pole," notes Fienberg.

Hence, to a present-day observer standing right on top of the North Pole, the North Celestial Pole appears directly overhead. And it's marked by—you guessed it—Polaris. It's because of this unique orientation that the entire northern sky seems to wheel around Polaris.

Let's say you put your Nikon digital astrophotography camera on a tripod and then point it up toward the heavens and leave the exposure open. "The stars leave trails as they appear to rotate around the sky," Fienberg explains. All the stars except Polaris, that is.

The North Star appears to stand perfectly still at the center of literally thousands of star arcs. Technically, Fienberg says, "Polaris does make a tiny trail." But it's really hard to see, so an everyday observer gets the impression that Polaris doesn't rise and set like its celestial counterparts. Of course, none of the stars are actually revolving around us. "As Earth rotates, the sky appears to move, and that's why it seems like stars rise and set," Fienberg points out.

If you stand outside for hours, watching the night sky, you wouldn't even need to locate the Big Dipper to track down Polaris. You could just figure out which star isn't moving. And to that end, the North Star can actually be a little bit useful for navigation. Polaris on its own, though, isn't going to save your you-know-what if you're lost at sea or stranded overnight in the woods.

An endless series of online resources provides some iteration of the following viewpoint: Way back in human history, people depended on their lucky stars for guidance while crossing open oceans and trackless wilderness.

"The constellations are quite ancient," Fienberg says, and yes, since the dawn of civilization, humans have probably used stars to assist with navigation. But here's the thing: Nobody relies solely on the night sky.

Finding Polaris means you know the way north if you're in the Northern Hemisphere. (Remember, from the Southern

Hemisphere you can't see Polaris because it's below the horizon.) So if you can see the North Star, and you're facing it, well then you know you're facing north. "You're looking toward the North Pole," Fienberg simplifies.

Face Polaris, stretch your arms out sideways, and you literally become a human compass. Your right hand points east, your left hand shoots west, and behind you, that's south. But knowing which way is north is only useful if you have other tools at your disposal.

It's a myth that a celestial navigator can find their way by relying solely on the stars.

Ancient Polynesian voyagers are famous for having navigated the Pacific Ocean by star, traveling thousands of miles without the aid of modern devices such as sextants and compasses. Constellations, though, weren't their only point of reference. The navigators relied on other "instruments of nature"—currents and seasonal winds, for example—to determine where they were headed when they couldn't see land in any direction. Imagine sitting in a dugout canoe about 1,000 years ago, traipsing from one archipelago to another, totally reliably, with only the sky, wind, and currents serving as your guide.

In the 1800s, fugitive slaves in the United States traveled undercover at night, usually without maps and compasses. They relied, instead, on the Big Dipper, often called the Drinking Gourd, to reveal—you guessed it!—Polaris, lighting their way to the free states up north. According to popular lore, travelers on the Underground Railroad looked for the Drinking Gourd and then followed the North Star to freedom. The Big Dipper and North Star were so important that they were mentioned in many slave narratives and songs, including "Follow the Drinking Gourd," a folksong composed decades after the American Civil War ended.

But American folk stories can be misleading. Even though they couldn't use formal navigational instruments, slaves had plenty of other way-finding aids, including rivers, roads, dead trees, and farmhouses—not to mention assistance from conductors stationed at designated meeting points along the route.

"Celestial navigation isn't just of historical interest, but remains useful during the Space Age," says Fienberg. All the Apollo crews, for example, used the stars to navigate to the moon and back.

So yes, stars can be really helpful, but if you're truly lost in the middle of nowhere, trying to find your way home, you're going to need more than just a bright star. You'll need to know your latitude and longitude. But luckily, Fienberg says, "The other thing Polaris is useful for is determining latitude."

Since the North Star always sits right above the North Pole, its height over the horizon can be used to calculate latitude, or one's distance from the equator. As you travel northward, Polaris climbs higher and higher in the sky, and if you go as far north as the North Pole, well, Polaris will appear directly overhead. The converse is also true: The farther south you go, the lower Polaris sinks toward the horizon.

Find the North Star, measure the angle between it and the horizon, and now you've got a second important data point: latitude. You're not out of the woods yet, though. "You still don't know your longitude," Fienberg says.

Longitude requires knowing the time and also which stars are on the celestial meridian at different times of night on different nights of the year. So please make sure to pack a reliable watch and a celestial almanac the next time you're planning to get lost in the wilderness! ("If you know the time and can identify a star on the meridian, consulting an almanac will immediately give you your longitude," Fienberg notes.)

Despite its shortcomings, Polaris makes for a good modern-day pole star. But it hasn't always been the North

Star, and it won't remain the North Star forever. A fainter star called Thuban, in the constellation Draco the Dragon, was the North Star when the Egyptians built the pyramids in 3000 BCE. And in another 12,000-ish years, Vega, a magnitude 0 star that's six or seven times brighter than Polaris, will be our pole star, at least for a while.

This part's a little complicated, but basically, Fienberg says, "Earth is tilted on its axis, which means its spin axis is not perpendicular to its orbital plane." This is what creates the seasons. "Just like a spinning top, the Earth wobbles, and that wobble is called precession," Fienberg continues.

Earth's precession takes roughly 26,000 years, which means that 13,000 years ago, the North Star was as far from the North Pole as it could get. "At different times during this 26,000-year cycle, different stars are closer to the North Celestial Pole," says Fienberg. Try not to worry about this too much. It's highly unlikely you'll be around to notice this major cosmic shift.

Just in case you're wondering, there's no comparable "pole" star in the Southern Hemisphere. "There's a faint star that's visible with the naked eye that's pretty darn close to the South Celestial Pole, but it's not bright, so you'd have to know your faint constellations in order to find it," says Fienberg.

Since navigating by star can be tricky business, your best bet is to avoid getting lost in the first place. While factors such as bad weather, injury, and darkness occasionally contribute to wilderness-related disappearances, wandering off the trail is the most common reason people get lost, according to Smokymountains.com, which examined more than 100 news reports of missing hikers.

Some recreationists travel off-trail because they're looking for shortcuts. In Colorado, for example, there's a 14,000-foot summit (Capitol Peak) that claims lives annually. Over the decades, many exhausted hikers have fallen to their deaths while attempting to take a shortcut on the descent. On less treacherous routes, a shortcut might not kill you right away, but it could get you hopelessly lost. Don't count on shortcuts to get you home. Be prepared for your hike with all the water and snacks you'll need to complete the route you're planning to tackle.

In the remote backcountry, some trails can be difficult to follow. But even when a trail is well marked, a seasoned outdoorsperson might still wander off the beaten path. Sometimes bushwhacking is just plain fun. And here's a tidbit that might surprise a few readers: It's totally possible to engage in off-trail navigation while still practicing Leave No Trace principles, says Ben Lawhon, senior director of research and consulting for the Leave No Trace Center for Outdoor Ethics.

That's right, it's a myth that good hikers should never wander off the trail.

When Lawhon and his family go backpacking, they'll often build off-trail segments into their planned route, "Just for the adventure of it," Lawhon says. If local land managers allow off-trail usage (always check first to be sure!), and you feel confident in your map-reading abilities, and the terrain is suitable . . . "Go for it," says Lawhon. Just make sure you're taking necessary steps to minimize your impact.

"When recreating in heavily used areas with trail networks, use the trails," Lawhon advises, explaining that designed trails are generally better for the environment since they're built to minimize impact.

However, continues Lawhon, outside of busy, frontcountry locations, "There are lots of places where it's totally appropriate to go off of the trail." Venture off-trail responsibly by sticking to the most durable surfaces available—rock, gravel, sand, and dry grass are all great choices. "People often forget about how durable grass is," Lawhon says, offering, "The research has consistently shown that dry grasses can be very durable surfaces." Broad leaf plants, on the other hand, might be permanently pulverized when trampled during just a few passes.

Once you've found the right surface, Lawhon says, "To the extent possible, have everyone in your group spread out to minimize footfall in a single area." The last thing you want to do is create a new trail.

There's one big exception to this general rule about fanning out: If you're traversing an area with living soil crust, formally called cryptobiotic soil crust, you literally want to step over everyone else's footprints to minimize impact, Lawhon explains. Found in desert regions including the Four Corners, Utah National Parks such as Canyonlands and Bryce Canyon, and Joshua Tree National Park in California, living soil crust is bumpy, clumpy, blackened soil made up of living things such as lichen, mosses, green algae, microfungi, and bacteria, but is dominated by cyanobacteria. "Tiptoe through the crypto," says Lawhon, offering an easy mnemonic device.

Assuming off-trail usage is permitted where you're recreating, make sure you have the wherewithal to try it safely. "Traveling off a trail is not without its challenges," Lawhon points out. While most hikers cover about 2 miles per hour traversing a man-made trail, your pace could slow to half-a-mile an hour once you've left the beaten path.

If you're planning to walk off-trail, you'll need to be self-sufficient. Do you have a map and compass, and can you use them? Could you survive for several days, and in poor weather, if you got lost? Do you know how to make a shelter? Are you carrying plenty of food and water? If you answer "no" to any of these questions, stick to the trails or go bushwhacking with an expert.

"We know for sure that rescues are very impactful," Lawhon says. When somebody is lost or injured in the backcountry, it takes a lot of manpower and money to get them out safely, and sometimes a rescue isn't possible.

Since cell phones don't always get service in remote areas, bushwhackers should consider carrying Personal Locator Beacons and Satellite Messengers for cutting-edge signaling options. And don't forget to pack a map, compass, watch, celestial almanac, and maybe even a sextant since the North Star will be useless for navigation without supplemental instruments.

BOTTOM LINE: The North Star isn't even close to being the brightest star in the night sky, and while locating Polaris will tell you which direction is north, you'll need additional information to navigate if you're lost outside at night. You're responsible for your own safety when recreating outdoors. It can be fun to bushwhack, but don't try it unless you're a pro at navigating the old-fashioned way, with a paper map and compass.

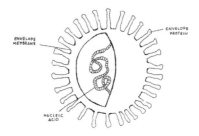

Here's How Cold Weather Really Impacts Human Health

"Oh, honey, get back here! You'll catch cold if you go outside with wet hair," my broad-shouldered Midwestern grand-mother wailed—on more than one occasion!—while chasing me through the house in mid-December, armed with a 1,000-watt Conair hair dryer and classic Denman brush, complete with the red base and pointed white bristles.

Maybe your hair was short, and so you avoided "the chase" altogether. Still, at some point during your childhood, you probably heard some version of the grandmotherly wisdom that you'd catch a cold from going outside in the cold with wet hair.

Some grandparents took it a step further, advis-ing against time outdoors in the cold with dry hair, too. Countless kids avoided drafty windows, over-bundled, and missed out on wintry adventures altogether—all in the name of good health. Now it's time to uncover the cold, hard truth about the relationship between cold weather and our im-mune systems.

This first tidbit probably won't surprise anyone since we've all been inundated with information from epidemiologists during the Covid-19 pandemic. Anyone with even the most basic knowledge of infectious disease can quickly dismiss my Grandma Marian's acuity.

It's definitely a myth that you'll catch a cold from being outside in the cold.

If you go outside in the cold with sopping wet hair, and then you bump into somebody who has, say, a rhinovirus (the cause of the common cold), you could definitely end up sick in bed in a couple of days. Your wet hair was inconsequential, though, because when it comes to infectious disease, it's germs that make us sick, not cold weather.

"We contract viruses from being in contact with other people," explains Sean O'Leary, MD, MPH, a pediatric infectious disease specialist and professor of pediatrics at Children's Hospital Colorado. "Some viruses," he continues, "are more contagious than others." But as a general rule of thumb, to catch a cold or the flu (a group of viruses known as influenza viruses), you'd have to be "in close contact—within several feet—of an infected person for more than a few minutes," O'Leary says.

There are exceptions to this rule, but none has anything to do with air temperature. "Some viruses," O'Leary notes, "are extremely contagious, like measles, where you could be across a large room—even a gymnasium—from someone who has it and still catch it." (Unless you are vaccinated against the measles, O'Leary points out, in which case you'd be protected.)

Other viruses can be picked up from direct contact, O'Leary continues. In this instance, a person gets sick by touching a surface where there is viable virus and then touching their face or rubbing their eyes. To reiterate: No, you cannot, you will not, catch a cold or the flu from recreating outside in cold weather—even if you forget to blow-dry your hair. But if this Old Wives' Tale is so easy to debunk, then how come colds and flus really do surge in the winter?

"Cold weather definitely plays a role in cold and flu season," O'Leary clarifies. Respiratory infections, in particular, circulate more frequently in the fall and winter months. In fact, most viruses have "seasonal patterns," as O'Leary puts it. And a number of factors probably contribute to these perennial spikes.

North American schools reopen in autumn, right around the time the mercury begins dropping in the Northern Hemisphere. So after a long, warm summer, people are spending more time indoors together, and according to the National Institute of Allergy and Infectious Diseases, both of these factors can increase one's exposure to diseases caused by viruses. The risk associated with cold weather, then, involves being inside around other people, not spending time outdoors.

"When it's cold outside," O'Leary says, "We tend to congregate indoors, where it's much easier to spread respiratory viruses. And the other piece," he continues, "is that certain viruses just seem to survive better in cold weather." In fact, many epidemiologists believe cold temperatures help viruses replicate more quickly and efficiently. But even this has more to do with atmospheric moisture than the temperature itself.

When temperatures plummet, the air gets drier, too, because cold air retains much less moisture than warm air. The warmer the air is, the more moisture it can potentially hold. And the more moisture in the air, the harder it is for viruses to grow.

When it's cold, on the other hand, moisture starts to precipitate, and "There's just not a lot of capacity for the colder air to hold water," explains geoscientist Elizabeth Gordon, professor and chair of Earth and Geographic Sciences at Fitchburg State University. That's why we stir sugar into sweet tea when the liquid's still hot.

Some research indicates that humidity actually hinders a virus's ability to replicate and spread, explaining why dry winter air has been linked to seasonal flu outbreaks. In 2010, for example, Dr. Jeffrey Shaman, PhD, of Oregon State University, along with collaborators at several other institutions, compared influenza death rates to absolute humidity readings.

In *PLoS Biology*, an open-access scientific journal, researchers reported "significant drops" in absolute humidity in the weeks leading up to flu outbreaks. "This dry period is not a requirement for triggering an influenza outbreak, but it was present in 55 to 60 percent of the outbreaks we analyzed, so it appears to increase the likelihood of an outbreak," Shaman wrote.

Two years earlier, scientists writing for *Nature Chemical Biology* speculated that the coating of a flu virus literally becomes tougher at near-freezing temperatures. (Picture an M&M melting in your hand on a warm day!) A tough outer layer, they found, makes flu viruses more resilient and much easier to transmit, explaining why winter is an optimal period for proliferation.

Rhinoviruses also seem to flourish at cooler temperatures. As your body's gateway to the upper respiratory tract, the nose's main job is to filter and clean air before it enters the lungs, which maintain a steady temperature around 98.6 degrees.

A human nose isn't quite so warm. Temperatures inside your nostrils will range from 91 to 95 degrees, and this cooler environment is a welcoming host for viruses causing the common cold. So much so that the pathogen's scientific name is drawn from its favorite hangout, *rhin*, a Greek prefix meaning the "nose."

A runny nose is the quintessential symptom of a common cold, yet cold weather often causes our noses to run, even when we aren't actually sick. It's not all in your head: "Chilly air means sniffly noses," wrote Deborah S. Clements, MD, a family medicine practitioner at the Northwestern Medical Group in Illinois.

Clements explained in a *Northwestern Medicine* blog post, "When we breathe in, our noses warm the air and add moisture to it as it travels down into our lungs. Cold, dry air irritates your nasal lining, and as a result, your nasal glands produce excess mucus to keep the lining moist."

If cold, dry air can prompt our bodies to make more mucus, can it also impact our ability to fight off an infection? Our bodies are lined with a bunch of thin, soft tissue called mucous membranes, which are designed to stop pathogens and dirt from entering the body, explains O'Leary. Viruses can penetrate membranes in places where they brush up against the skin—think: eyes, mouth, ears, and nose.

Cold and flu viruses usually enter the body through the eyes, nose, or mouth and progress into the lungs from there. Our nasal hair and snot function like frontline soldiers, offering an initial defense against invaders. But, according to some researchers, cold weather dries out the inside lining of the nose, impairing nasal hair and mucus, making it easier for viruses to slip past the body's natural defenses. If you want to avoid catching a cold or the flu this winter, you could try using saline nasal spray or a humidifier in your bedroom.

Your best bet, though, is to practice good hygiene, including frequent hand washing. "As far as I'm aware, the only safeguard that has any basis in evidence is hand washing," O'Leary says, noting that homeopathic tactics involving saline sprays and humidity really haven't been studied enough yet to be recommended for prevention, although they can definitely provide comfort if you become sick this winter.

What if you get really cold from spending time out of doors? "Some researchers have also theorized that if you become hypothermic, it might suppress your immune system, making you more susceptible to infection," adds O'Leary.

In 2015, researchers used a mouse-adapted virus to see if, similar to the rhinovirus itself, the human immune system is also easily affected by fluctuations in the body's internal thermostats. After removing cells from mouse airways and incubating them at two different temperatures (91 degrees and 98.6 degrees), researchers found that the cells stored in a warmer environment launched a more robust attack than the ones kept at cooler temperatures.

Findings were published in *Proceedings of the National Academy of Sciences,* where the researchers stated, "Cooler temperatures can enable replication of the common cold virus, at least in part, by diminishing antiviral immune responses." Or in laymen's terms, exposure to cold air might hinder your body's natural ability to fight off an infection. More research is needed to confirm these findings, so please don't put off your backcountry hut trip just yet, and definitely don't keep your children inside all winter.

Looking at the flip side of the coin, since the mid-1990s, scientists have also been studying whether cold exposure could potentially *bolster* the body's ability to fight infections by activating the immune system.

In 1996 a team of researchers explored the impact a single cold-water immersion had on the immune systems of young male athletes. Participants plunged into frigid, 14-degree Celsius (57.2 degrees Fahrenheit) water where they stayed for an hour. By monitoring them immediately before and after the immersion, scientists discovered that changes in their immune functions were minimal with a single cold-water dip.

But with the continuation of cold-water immersions (three times a week for a duration of six weeks), a small increase in the proportions of monocytes and lymphocytes with expressed IL2 receptors was induced. In the *European Journal of Applied Physiology,* researchers concluded, "Stress-inducing noninfectious stimuli, such as repeated cold-water immersions, which increased metabolic rate due to shivering . . . activated the immune system to a slight extent."

In a cold environment, most adults will shiver to generate heat by rapidly tightening and relaxing their muscles. Human babies, though, aren't able to shiver, so they're born with brown adipose tissue, or BAT, an insulin-sensitive tissue packed with iron-rich mitochondria. Mitochondria are "the heart of your cells," says Lindy Rossow, PhD, assistant professor of Exercise Science at Maryville University of St. Louis. "Mitochondria take in nutrients like sugar and white fat and break them down to make energy," she adds.

Simply put, "Brown fat is more metabolically active than white fat," Rossow continues, describing white fat as "an inert tissue that just sits there," storing your energy in large fat droplets. White fat is made of big droplets of lipids, or fatty acids, the fat that stores up in the thighs, hips, and tummy.

Excess white fat is associated with all sorts of health problems, from heart disease to diabetes. Brown fat, by contrast, generates heat like a built-in space heater. It's the same fat that bears use to stay warm when they hibernate.

We all lose the majority of the brown fat we were born with as we age because we learn how to shiver. Once you can shiver, you don't really need brown fat to keep you warm anymore. Adults retain some brown fat in the neck and upper back, but it's not something you can build like muscle. When it comes to staying warm in the cold, Rossow points out that, "Any tissue, even white fat, will keep you warm, but muscle is especially beneficial because it contracts to help you shiver."

In his book *What Doesn't Kill Us: How Freezing Water, Extreme Altitude, and Environmental Conditioning Will Renew Our Lost Evolutionary Strength*, journalist Scott Carney looks at research surrounding brown fat while presenting a detailed dive into a possible link between extreme cold temperatures and enhanced human health. Carney investigated Dutch extreme athlete Wim Hof, who is known worldwide for his ability to withstand freezing temperatures.

Hof claims that cold exposure improves immune function. According to him, cold weather doesn't make us sick. Rather, short, targeted exposures to ultra-cold environments, Hof claims, can actually support overall health by activating brown fat and reawakening primal instincts that are typically suppressed by modern life.

Most of us aren't spending prolonged periods of time in cold environments. Thanks to synthetic fabrics, Carney says, "People can dress to maintain their indoor temperature." In the winter in his hometown in Colorado, Carney resists modern technology by running a few miles shirtless in 0-degree weather. "It's uncomfortable for the first five minutes," he says. "But for a short run, it's not going to kill you." If you take Hof's word for it, it might even make you healthier.

It's worth mentioning that the Wim Hof Method has been fatal to some practitioners, mostly those mixing his breathing method with underwater exposure. Hof himself has almost died—several times—while swimming below ice. And of course, when it comes to prolonged cold exposure, outdoors enthusiasts have some real ailments to consider, mainly hypothermia and frostbite. "Maybe you're not going to catch a cold if you're stranded outside in December, but if you get hypothermia, you could die," Rossow says.

It's not a good idea to try anything new without first seeking approval from a licensed medical doctor, so definitely don't start plunging into frigid water on account of Hof and this book. If you're going to experiment with cold exposure, your best bet is to work with a trained expert.

While Rossow remains skeptical of Hof's claims that humans can become healthier by activating BAT, she agrees that healthier people tend to have more robust immune systems. Rossow says adults who'd like to be healthy should focus on exercise and a good diet versus cold exposure.

BOTTOM LINE: Viruses make us sick. While cold weather might help viruses replicate and spread, external temperatures probably don't do much to negatively impact our immune systems. Some scientific outliers believe short exposure to extremely cold temperatures could make people healthier, but at the very least, playing outside in the cold is less risky than staying cooped up indoors with other people's germs.

The Fungus among Us

Next time you're in an old-growth forest, listen for the downy woodpecker hammering away at the trunk of a deciduous tree. Follow the sound until you locate, say, a 75-foot-tall sugar maple, or maybe it's a white elm with insects hiding inside the rough bark.

Now follow the tree's thick trunk down to the forest floor. Look past your waterproof hiking boots, study the ground, observe clumps of grass, dirt, fallen leaves—maybe a few mushrooms, too, if you're looking closely enough.

You know those glass-bottomed boats designed to enhance fish viewing? Just imagine if somebody installed a transparent pane directly onto the ground. Suddenly you'd be able to see the intricate, lively, concealed world right below the topsoil, which claims miles and miles of fungi spread across a network that looks about as labyrinthine as a Tokyo subway map.

Mushrooms are cryptic, to say the least, explains Andrew Wilson, PhD, assistant curator of mycology at the Denver Botanic Gardens. When we eat fungi, we're consuming the organism's flowering reproductive structure. "We rarely see the organism itself because it's under the ground or inside wood," adds mycologist Michael Beug, professor emeritus at Evergreen State College and a top expert on morels.

In fact, the vast majority of fungi lives underground and is composed of all these weird, white tendrils. "They're little threads, smaller than an eyelash," says Wilson, kind of like cobwebs or "branching networks of silk," Wilson adds. This is the mycelium.

The mycelium branches out and grows in every direction, creating a three-dimensional formation some scientists claim has more networks than a human brain has neural pathways. What's really amazing is that trees in a forest can exchange nutrients via underground mycelia, and plants also use mycelium grids to communicate, leading some cheeky mycologists to nickname mycelia the wood wide web. Though she wasn't the first scientist to observe symbiotic relationships between plants and fungi, biologist Suzanne Simard was "instrumental," says Beug, in deepening the scientific community's understanding of these mycorrhizal partnerships.

Many people wrongly assume that mushrooms are plants.

"Mushrooms are largely associated with plants," Wilson says, pointing out that mushrooms come from the ground, and we eat them. In fact, researchers have found that "fungi so thoroughly infiltrate the roots of most every plant in the wild that they are inextricable from the plants themselves." It kind of makes sense, then, that mushrooms and other fungi were included in the Plant Kingdom for a really long time, until the late 1970s or early 1980s, Beug says.

"But biologically speaking, mushrooms are in their own kingdom, the kingdom fungi," Wilson explains, which includes yeasts, rusts, smuts, mildews, and molds. Beug says, "I have not found the exact date, but by sometime in the 1980s, fungi were recognized as a fifth kingdom." He adds, "And by

2000, seven kingdoms were recognized," prompting Bryce Kendrick to update his beloved book, *The Fifth Kingdom*, for a third time.

Fungi are thought to be one of the oldest forms of life. And after studying fungi DNA, scientists now know that fungi are much more similar to animals than plants. Animals divided from fungi about 650 million years ago. That's why Beug says, "Fungi appear at the base of the tree from which animals arose, a completely different branch from which flowering plants arose."

When they split, animals evolved to digest their food internally, whereas fungi decided instead to digest theirs externally before absorbing it. That's one of the key differences between fungi and animals. But in other ways, fungi are just like us!

"Like animals, fungi need to feed to gain energy," Wilson explains. "This energy comes from food, which is supplied by and large by plants," he adds. Fungi need plants to survive.

Plants are "primary producers," taking the sun's energy and converting it into glucose, a form of energy nonproducers can use. Since fungi lack chlorophyll, they can't convert the sun's energy into food. But fungi aren't total free loaders: They pull their weight by developing symbiotic relationships with producers, giving trees and other plants minerals in exchange for glucose.

Fungi are really crafty sometimes. They have the ability to mine through root and rock, and some are even meat-eaters, hunting for flea-sized insects including springtails and nematodes. "Fungi are probably more diverse than any other group. They're definitely more diverse than plants, and we believe they are more diverse than animals," Wilson notes. As such, scientists are constantly learning new things about fungi, and they're continually making novel identifications, too, which can be really exciting in the Information Age, when it sometimes seems like Google already knows everything.

Right now, estimates based on high-throughput sequencing methods suggest that as many as 5.1 million fungal species exist. But by the time this book comes out, that figure will surely be outdated.

Not all fungi produce mushrooms—that is, fruiting bodies that materialize in all sorts of interesting shapes and colors, including bioluminescent varietals. Even though mushrooms and poisonous mushrooms (sometimes called "toadstools" by nonscientists) might not be the most plentiful fungi, they're definitely the easiest to spot.

Scientists can get nitpicky with definitions, but at the most basic level, Beug explains, "Fungi technically have to have gills to be called a mushroom." A morel, then, isn't really a mushroom. "But that's purely a technicality," Beug says, adding, "From a practical standpoint, I refer to morels as mushrooms. Any fungus that's large and fleshy, we tend to call a mushroom."

"Fungi are really kind of odd," Wilson says. Wildlife biologists can watch herds of elk roam a mountain meadow, and since most vegetation needs sunlight to grow, botanists can easily observe the lives of plants unfolding aboveground. But with fungi, Wilson points out, "The vast majority of their interactions with nature are hidden from observation." We can only see "the indirect consequences of their actions," as he puts it. So when mushrooms do pop up, it almost seems "magical," Wilson says, because they appear out of nowhere.

This might help to explain why there's no shortage of myths and misconceptions surrounding mushrooms. "Because mushrooms are so mysterious, they lend themselves to rumors, fantasies, and general mythology," Wilson speculates.

In her field guide *Mushrooms of the Upper Midwest*, mycologist Kathy Yerich and co-author Teresa Marrone include a laundry list of mushroom-related myths ranging from cooking strategies (i.e., cooking a mushroom with a silver coin eliminates poison—false!) to purported "tips" for easy identification, including the Old Wives' Tale that all poisonous mushrooms are brightly colored (also false).

"While foragers certainly take into account a mushroom's color during identification, there are tons of other factors to ponder," says Yerich, offering quite a list of considerations: shape, texture, the presence of gills, spore color, cap placement, growth patterns, and even what the mushroom is growing on.

A very common fungi misconception is that mushrooms are safe to eat when they smell good or seem visually appealing.

The genus *Amanita* contains about 600 species of fruiting fungi with mushrooms that tend to be "beautiful and charismatic," Wilson says. Beware: The genus is also known for containing 60 of the world's most deadly species, all closely related to the common and highly toxic *Amanita phalloides*, which is filled with amatoxins (a subgroup of at least nine related toxic compounds).

You wouldn't know it from the taste, though. "Most, if not all sixty, of these deadly species are incredibly delicious," Beug says. *Amanita phalloides* is the most widespread, though, and thus the most commonly eaten species, explaining how people end up being sickened by the so-called "destroying angel."

It's a myth that cooking mushrooms can reveal toxicity.

Other mushroom mores focus on preparation versus identification. According to one folk method, rice turns red when it's cooked with poisonous mushrooms. Do not—I repeat, do not—trust any quick-tricks regarding mushroom preparation. "Most toxins will have no effect whatsoever on silver or rice," says Beug. And while some toxins can be destroyed with heat, others aren't impacted at all by frying, baking, grilling, or boiling.

"There are so many mushroom species that learning about what is edible can be overwhelming," Yerich says, adding, "Everyone is looking for an easy trick, and over time there are definitely tricks that have emerged for making certain species less toxic." Yerich guesses that these various tips for detoxifying specific species have been passed down over generations and then applied in general to all mushrooms, thus becoming myths.

As different cultures throughout history concocted various practices for selecting wild mushrooms and preparing them safely, foraging traditions were passed down by many gener ations, even before European colonizers brought their fungi folk methods to North America. Since North America is "a melting pot of many cultures," says Beug, it's also a place where many mushroom myths have just sort of fused together.

While some Native American tribes used foraged mushrooms for food, "many tribes associated mushrooms with death and did not have a tradition of eating them," Beug notes. To this day, there are plenty of people who fear all mushrooms across the board, linking even the most delectable edible fruits with death and dying. Fungi are decomposers, so associating them with demise isn't totally off base. Essentially, fungi are the "digestive tracts of the forest," says Wilson, breaking down rotting plants and animals to clear a path for new life.

Mushrooms aren't as dangerous as reports from many mainstream news outlets suggest.

A few types of mushrooms could definitely kill you, and those species grab all the headlines. In reality, though, the vast majority of identified mushrooms are harmless. "Offhand, I'd say about 90 percent of all mushrooms are innocuous," Beug says, meaning they aren't dangerous, but they aren't all that interesting to eat either. There are plenty of nonculinary mushrooms that won't harm you. "They're just not tasty," Wilson explains, adding, "They're edible, but not delectable."

Of the remaining 10 percent of identified mushrooms, a handful make up the delicious, culinary species, the so-called "choice edibles." These mushrooms can be extremely healthful and nutritious. A research study from Penn State suggested that people who consumed 18 grams of mushrooms daily had a 45 percent lower risk of cancer than people who didn't eat mushrooms. The researchers credit an antioxidant in mushrooms called ergothioneine for this anticancer boost, and they noted that shiitake, oyster, maitake, and king oyster varietals have higher amounts of ergothioneine than white button, cremini, and Portobello mushrooms, the latter of which are all varieties of the species *Agaricus bisporus*, says Wilson.

Not all mushrooms will make you healthier, though. A few identified mushrooms are toxic, and these varieties can make people violently sick. So how can you tell the difference between edible and toxic mushrooms?

"Many culinary mushrooms are very distinctive," says Beug. But you'll need to have a good book to tell you what to look for and whether there are similar toxic species. "That is why I wrote *Mushrooms of Cascadia: An Illustrated Key*, a book for beginners and experts alike, designed to be very useful even outside of the Cascadia bioregion," Beug adds.

But here's the disclaimer: While many toxic mushrooms are distinctive—*if you know what to look for*—there are some look-alikes, that is, toxic species that could potentially be confused with edible mushrooms. This is where amateur foragers can get into real trouble. "The important thing is to learn which of the culinary mushrooms have look-alikes that are toxic, and to stay away from those culinary mushrooms until you are very experienced," Beug says.

Mushroom foraging is having a major renaissance in North America right now, and you can safely partake in this thrilling, outdoor hobby. The message isn't to fear mushrooms. Yet, it's important to educate yourself and use common sense when foraging anything in the wild.

Some plants also have very deadly toxins. If you were to go out plant picking, and you ate any and every plant you found, you could die "far more easily than by eating any mushroom you find," Beug says, adding, "Just as it is safe for a reasonably observant person to go blackberry picking, it's safe to go shaggy mane picking or chanterelle picking."

Toxins involved in mushroom poisonings are produced naturally by the fungi themselves. "Fungi are specifically adapted to break down the excess carbon in our environment," Wilson says, adding, "They are experts at consuming free carbon produced by plants—for example, wood—and converting it into a nutrient source." Because fungi are such a diverse species, different fungi interact with nature in different ways. "They can consume all types of substances," notes Wilson, and their bodies metabolize carbon in different ways. "Mushrooms are massive chemical factories," according to Beug. "A lot of times they have evolved because, presumably, the production of a certain chemical benefited them," he says.

Fungi reproduce by spreading their spores, and the main purpose of the fruit-body (i.e., the mushroom) is to produce spores. Wind will often carry lightweight mushroom spores, but some species rely on animals to help them reproduce by eating and digesting their reproductive structure then pooping it out. In this animal-dispersal scenario, fungi don't want to be consumed until their spores are mature. And even then, fungi really only want to be consumed by the right animals, ones that will be able to scatter their spores in favorable habitats.

Animal spore dispersal helps explain away the myth that if you see an animal or insect eating a mushroom, then you know it's safe to consume.

Many animals, including insects, can safely eat mushrooms that would severely harm or kill a human. In fact, Beug says,

"Even though the vast majority of mushroom-related human deaths are caused by amatoxin consumption, there are classes of mammals that can consume amatoxins without getting sick. Ditto for insects."

There are actually tons of rodents, including squirrels, with the ability to detoxify and digest amatoxins. Humans, dogs, and horses, though, do not have the same aptitude. Instead, the protein wreaks havoc on our mortal livers. With treatment from a knowledgeable doctor, though, Beug estimates that 90 percent of people will survive amatoxin poisoning.

It probably won't be pretty. Symptoms of mushroom poisoning vary based on the type of mushroom consumed. Some toxins cause organ failure, while others set off neurological symptoms. Mushroom poisoning may even be implicated in ALS (Lou Gehrig's disease). Many toxins bring about gnarly gastrointestinal issues, including nausea, severe stomach cramping, vomiting, and diarrhea, the latter of which can land victims in the emergency room with dehydration. If you eat a toxic mushroom, you might also end up with a headache, high blood pressure, or hallucinations. And some patients don't encounter any immediate side effects but will experience kidney damage that's so bad they need a transplant to survive.

When it comes to toxic mushroom ingestion, timing is everything. If GI troubles appear 6 to 24 hours after consumption, then beware: "This can be a signal that you've ingested amatoxins," Beug says. If you're in North America, though, you should survive with emergency medical intervention. "With amatoxins, the most important thing to do is hook up the patient to an IV and push fluids," Beug notes. The idea is that you'll pee the toxin out before it kills you.

Freaked out yet? Don't be. It's totally safe to walk through the forest.

There's also a myth that merely touching a toxic mushroom can make somebody ill.

That's false—no need to wear gloves or any protective clothing while foraging for mushrooms. "There's no mushroom I wouldn't put in my mouth, chew, and then spit out," says Beug, adding that, "There are much more poisonous things that we keep in our houses, often under the kitchen sink."

Mass mushroom poisonings definitely happen, and people do get sick from eating toxic mushrooms. Not as often as you'd think, though, and in North America, it's actually pretty rare for somebody to die from eating a poisonous mushroom since advanced medical care is typically available. There are about thirty poison centers in the United States and Canada, Beug estimates, and each center gets anywhere from 100 to 1,000 suspected mushroom poisoning cases per year. "A huge percentage are mushroom scares, not poisonings," Beug clarifies.

Hospitalizations in the United States due to mushroom poisoning are very uncommon. There is typically just a handful per year per poison center, even in regions where foraging is widely practiced. "The average number of reported mushroom poisoning deaths in the U.S. and Canada combined tends to be about one death per year," adds Beug.

One confusing thing is that allergies to mushrooms often produce the same symptoms that would indicate a poisonous reaction. "Edible mushrooms are very nutritious, but they also have very unusual proteins that some people react to," explains Beug, observing that, "There's virtually no food on Earth that some people don't react to."

If you're into edible mushrooms, and you're looking for a reliable trick to follow, here's one: Never eat a raw mushroom. Some mushrooms contain a carcinogen called hydrazine that will evaporate under heat, and other mushrooms might be contaminated with heat-sensitive bacteria. So even if you're currently riding the raw food craze, Beug says, "All mushrooms should be well-cooked, with truffles as the exception since they are used in tiny amounts like a spice."

Here's a quick note on psilocybin mushrooms.

There are a lot of myths and misconceptions surrounding magic mushrooms, and scientific inquiry continues. But that's as far as we're going here.

BOTTOM LINE: Mushrooms aren't plants, they're fungi, and the whole Fungi Kingdom is having a major renaissance right now. While some mushrooms can be extremely nutritive, a few could kill you. Folk methods of identification are not safe, so unless you're a mushroom expert, forage with somebody who knows what they're doing, or simply buy your mushrooms from a store or farmers' market and cook them well before consuming them.

Wolves, Explained

Today's *Final Jeopardy* answer (in the category "Wolves"): The number of humans killed by wolves in the contiguous United States in the last 100 years.

Question: What is zero?

That's right, in the last century exactly zero people have been killed and eaten by wolves in the lower 48 states. And if you wanted to add in Alaska and Canada, to include all of North America, there have been only two human deaths caused by wolves in that time frame, says wolf biologist L. David Mech, a top wolf expert and senior research scientist with the US Geological Survey. To put that number into context, domestic dogs kill about thirty Americans annually.

It's definitely a myth that wolves prey on people.

Yet, Hollywood filmmakers routinely portray the world's largest canine as a man-eater. "This better not be one of those movies where everyone gets eaten by wolves," I've said to my spouse, more than once, while settling in on the couch for screenings of *The Grey* (2011), *Wolf Town* (2011), and *Frozen*

(2010). (No, no—not that *Frozen*, not the sweet Disney musical from 2013. The other movie, the one where a group of skiers is stranded on a ski lift and forced to survive overnight with a hungry pack of wolves at their toes.)

Spoiler alert: When wolves are on the silver screen, it's almost always one of those movies where everyone gets eaten.

The wild, mournful sound of wolves howling under the glow of the moon makes good horror movie fodder, to be sure, and wolves have also inspired a slew of fictional childhood classics: "Little Red Riding Hood," "The Three Little Pigs," and Aesop's fable about "The Boy Who Cried Wolf."

But if wolves don't actually eat people, why is that such a prevalent theme in fiction? How did they become the archetypal storybook villain?

"Wolves have killed people," Mech says. "It doesn't happen often," he adds. Wolf-related deaths are more common in present-day India, Mech notes, where young children in rural farming communities have occasionally been taken while playing alone in fields. But even that's a pretty uncommon occurrence.

"Our fear of wolves stems back to religion and mythology," according to Erika Moore, an animal care supervisor at the Colorado Wolf and Wildlife Center, one of America's few wolf sanctuaries certified by the Association of Zoos and Aquariums (AZA). In addition to the popular fairy tales, fables, folklore, and mythology, the Bible, too, Moore says, portrays wolves in a devilish way, ultimately feeding into the myth that wolves are bloodthirsty monsters.

Wolves have wandered North America for 10,000 to 130,000 years, chasing prey at 35-plus miles per hour, gnawing meals with big teeth set inside powerful jaws. Just like dogs and other canines, a wolf's teeth are strong and sharp. After chasing prey, wolves use their jaws to bite their catch, causing massive bleeding. Death by wolf would be a terrible way to go, and even though wolves don't prey on people, they personify our mortal fear of suffering a painful death.

While some online resources mention a symbiotic relationship between wolves and early humans living 12,000 years ago, Mech can't confirm these claims. "Generally wolves and humans were enemies for millennia," he says, pointing out that "each was capable of killing the other."

Observations of wolves dating back to the Dark Ages have only heightened our innate fear of these animals, while perpetuating the misconception that wolves prey on people. Like all mammals, wolves can carry the virus that causes rabies, an often-fatal brain disease. Throughout medieval times, some rabid wolves did, in fact, attack humans. Watching in horror, onlookers failed to make the connection between their behavior and the disease, Mech says.

As the bubonic plague peaked in Europe between 1347 and 1351, "people died so quickly that survivors couldn't properly bury the dead," Moore continues. Those who were spared from the illness set up mass graves on the outskirts of cities, and these sites ended up being "a free buffet for wildlife," as Moore puts it. All predators and scavengers took advantage of an easy food source, and yet for whatever reason, wolves caught a bad rap. Europeans saw wolves preying on the bodies of deceased loved ones, and their imaginations ran wild.

Before the Industrial Revolution, wild wolves lived throughout most of the continental United States. In the 1600s, Moore says, an estimated 250,000 wolves called America home. Farming, though, put a permanent strain on the relationship between humans and wolves, and if there was a nail-in-the-coffin moment, that probably came during the Agricultural Revolution.

When European colonists failed to fence their livestock in the New World, sheep and cattle became such easy targets for wild wolves that the burgeoning American government issued wolf bounties, heightening our fear of wolves while launching a massive government wolf extermination program in the lower 48 states. During the 1800s, and even into the

1900s, wolves were hunted to near-extinction. By the 1960s, there were only 500 to 750 gray wolves left in the continental United States, all living in Minnesota.

Wolves were placed on the Endangered Species List in 1967. A few years later, in 1973, the Endangered Species Act became law, and killing wolves was illegal. America's wolf population has since been reestablished. "There are now at least 6,000 wolves in the lower 48 states," says Mech, and all wolves except for the Mexican Gray Wolf were taken off the Endangered Species List in January of 2021.

Policies have changed since the nineteenth century, but wolves are still getting into some trouble with livestock. Wolves prey on hoofed animals, Mech explains, and while deer and elk are their sustenance of choice, cows and sheep also have hooves. Some wolves have made headlines for taking domesticated animals.

This next bit is controversial among wildlife biologists, experts, and activists, and it's created political rifts in some parts of the country. According to Mech, "A well-regulated, government-run hunting season on gray wolves can help mitigate problems with livestock depredations." Specialists like Moore respectfully disagree, arguing that domesticated livestock are not a wolf's primary food source.

Montana, Idaho, and Wyoming are the three contiguous US states with the vast majority of wild wolves. More than six million head of cattle live in this western tristate region, making it a pretty good place to study the interaction between wolves and livestock.

US Fish and Wildlife Service reports show that in 2014, in Montana, Idaho, and Wyoming, wolves killed 136 head of cattle, or 1 cow out of every 44,853. In the same three states in 2014, wolves killed 114 sheep, or 1 in every 7,193. Losses can be unevenly distributed, sometimes taking a big toll on individual ranchers. "Nobody wants to be that one rancher who is impacted disproportionately," Moore says.

Yet, according to Moore, "The lethal management of wolves is ineffective." She points to a research article, "Effects of Wolf Mortality on Livestock Depredations," published in 2014 in *PLoS ONE*, an open-access, peer-reviewed journal. In their discussion, the authors of the study wrote, "Lethal control of wolves appears to be related to increased depredations in a larger area the following year." Findings indicated that ranchers who used preventative techniques to manage wolves, as opposed to lethal management, lost less livestock over time.

The article is compelling on first glance, but several additional articles appear in the same journal, and they challenge the purported findings laid out in "Effects of Wolf Mortality on Livestock Depredations." Many wolf advocates will cite the original article without citing the articles challenging it, Mech points out.

Mech has studied wolves for over 60 years, and there's more to wolves than stock-raising politics. While a cattle rancher might need to worry about wolves, outdoors enthusiasts can breathe a big sigh of relief. The statistics simply don't support the notion that wolves are dangerous man-eaters. Even when recreating in remote wilderness areas, outdoors fans really don't have to worry about wolves. "You can hike in Yellowstone," Mech says. And that's not just a random location he's referencing.

In 1995, after 20 years of planning, 31 wolves were relocated from Canada into the Greater Yellowstone Ecosystem. They were the first wolves reintroduced into the ecosystem in 75 years. As of 2019, biologists counted roughly 100 to 125 wolves across eight packs living throughout Yellowstone's nearly 3,500-square-mile wilderness. Some people are now under the (mistaken) impression that wolves run rampant throughout the park. But that's a pretty small figure given the size of the area, Mech notes. According to him, it would be unusual for a hiker to see a wolf while hiking inside Yellowstone, yet common for that same hiker to drive through the park and spot a wolf. "There are people who find wolves each day along the roads and watch them with scopes," he notes.

If this gives you goose bumps, keep in mind that most ecological communities are healthiest when they are balanced. "Wolf reintroduction, along with the recovery of other carnivores, has helped restore the park ecosystem by increasing natural predation," explains wildlife biologist Doug Smith, the project leader for the Wolf Restoration Project in Yellowstone. Inside Yellowstone, wolves are having a cascading impact on the park-wide food chain, helping to increase beaver populations and bring back aspens and other vegetation.

Although you probably won't see a wolf while you're out recreating, you could definitely come across a coyote. "They're found all over the United States, often in cities," Mech says, adding, "Coyotes are like smaller wolves." Weighing in at 20 to 30 pounds, this species of canine is about one-third the size of a typical wolf, but can look remarkably similar to its close relative. The two animals evolved from the same common ancestor and can actually interbreed, though they rarely do in the wild.

Because coyotes are common, and because they inhabit dense, urban areas, there are more reports of coyotes injuring people and their pets. If you see a coyote in the wild, never run, no matter how nervous you feel. Try to avoid an encounter altogether by altering your course. If that doesn't work, and the coyote approaches, you should "haze" it by yelling in an angry voice, waving your arms in the air, and throwing rocks and sticks in its direction. Hazing can help to maintain a coyote's natural fear of humans.

The same hazing method should be used to fend off wild wolves, although it's highly unlikely you'd ever have to employ it since wolves so rarely approach humans. While there are thousands of gray wolves living in the United States today, their current range is much smaller than that of coyotes, limited to portions of just 10 of the lower 48 states plus Alaska, mostly due to the fact that their habitats have been destroyed in many parts of the country.

Minnesota currently claims the largest wolf population, with about 2,600 of the canines, give or take. "Idaho has around 1,000 wolves," Mech continues, adding that, "The main population, outside of Minnesota, is in a region comprised of Idaho, Montana, Wyoming, Oregon, Washington, and Northern California." Combined, those states have an estimated 4,000 wolves, and in Alaska there are anywhere from 8,000 to 10,000. But Canada takes the cake, claiming around 60,000 wolves, Mech estimates.

There are three species of wolf worldwide, and two exist in the United States. While red wolves are found only in a small area of coastal North Carolina, gray wolves have a wider range and include several subspecies: the arctic wolf, northwestern wolf, Great Plains wolf, Mexican wolf, and the eastern timber wolf (debated by some as a distinct species). Any differences among the types are so minor that they're meaningless to most people, except a few specialists like Mech.

An average-size North American male gray wolf weighs from 70 to 130 pounds, stands 26 to 36 inches at the shoulders, and stretches 5 to 6 feet from nose to the tip of the tail. "Females are about 20 percent smaller," Mech says, and the coat or fur of a gray wolf can range dramatically, from gray to tan, brown, rusty red, or even bright white.

When it comes to their physical traits (large teeth, jaws with enough bite force to crush a moose's thighbone), wolves are definitely top-level carnivores with the ability to harm humans. But wild wolves are shy and generally avoid people. "We almost extinguished wolves while settling America," Moore points out. "This played a big, enduring role in wolf behavior," she continues, adding, "Wolves look at people as a threat."

When you're hiking through wolf habitat, you won't have any idea where the wolves are, but they'll know exactly where you are. "They're keeping a nice, safe distance," Moore says, adding that "they don't want a conflict." If you see a wolf in the wild, that wolf is letting you see it.

Humans are the third major cause of death of wild wolves, after disease and starvation, Moore explains. With an average lifespan of just four to six years, most wild wolves have high mortality rates, though wolves living in captivity can survive up to 17 years. Wild wolves really do live in packs. Unless you've studied wolves extensively, though, you probably have some misconceptions about the pack structure.

"The important thing to understand is that a pack is usually a family consisting of a pair of adult wolves and their offspring," Mech says. That's right, wolf packs are just families, and a normal, healthy pack mimics our nuclear human families, consisting of a mom and dad living with the kiddos.

Mother wolves give birth, usually every year, to an average litter of six, and the pups live with their parents for about two years, sometimes three, until they're mature enough to disperse from the pack, find a mate, and start their own clan. Every once in a while, you'll see a pack with an older wolf, an aunt or a grandma, maybe, who really enjoys hanging out with the family and decided to stick around.

Similar to humans, Mom and Dad run the family, dictating who goes where and when. To have a successful wolf pack—and success is defined as being able to catch sufficient food—you need at least four wolves. The largest pack ever recorded, though, had 42 wolves, Mech notes. "We take a lot of information from Yellowstone, where an average pack size is ten to fifteen wolves," adds Moore.

Many people erroneously think that the pack structure makes hunting a breeze. "You'd think a pack of five wolves could very easily take down a deer or a moose, but in fact their success rate is very low," Mech says. The idea that wolves can easily kill anything they want is totally inaccurate. "And you can just forget the term 'alpha' completely," Mech continues, adding, "We biologists don't use that word anymore."

The concept of an "alpha wolf" is a misinterpretation of an obsolete experiment.

The term "alpha" is an obnoxiously enduring nod to a 1940s wolf behavior study—"Expression Studies on Wolves"—conducted by German behaviorist Rudolph Schenkel. Basically, Schenkel captured a bunch of wolves from different packs and then threw them together in captivity with the goal of studying wild wolf behavior. Up until that point, biologists really hadn't studied wolves, and Schenkel had no idea that wolves live in family structures and are also extremely territorial.

Moore prefers to think of wolves as "family oriented" and explains that "outside their packs, they generally don't get along with other wolves." If two packs come across each other in the wild, there's going to be a brawl. So when Schenkel united a bunch of wild wolves from different packs, it was sort of like MTV's reality TV series *The Real World*, except that all the actors had these very scary teeth. Schenkel watched in awe as his subjects battled one another while establishing a pecking order.

Mech fills in the rest of the details, explaining, "Schenkel called the top wolf the alpha, and since his study was the first of its kind, it got a lot of attention." Even though Schenkel was completely wrong about alphas, the term stuck. "The public still doesn't understand that in the wild, that's simply not how it works," Mech notes, offering, "Rank order in a wolf pack is just about the same as in a human family." Essentially, the breeding pair of wolves will dominate their offspring until their offspring are mature enough to disperse from the pack.

Pack structure is not the only thing we laypeople get wrong about wolves. A quick Google search reveals at least 4,525 stock images of disembodied wolf heads howling at a full moon.

Sorry, but it's a myth that wolves howl at the moon.

In fact, wolves aren't even nocturnal. "They're crepuscular," Moore says, explaining, "They are most active at dawn and dusk, and they generally sleep through the night and nap during the day."

The myth that wolves howl at the moon probably developed slowly over time, Mech guesses. During a full moon, many animals are hyperactive, taking advantage of the extra light to hunt for food. And much like your pet dog, wolves communicate with barks and howls. Time for dinner? Mom sends out a howl to rally the group for a hunt.

Packs can have a territory of 300-plus square miles. That's a pretty large hunting ground. "Just imagine trying to communicate with your family over long distances while gathering your dinner," Moore says, adding, "This is where howling becomes super important."

Howling is the most direct way of communicating across long distances. During a hunt, wolves might split up while chasing different prey. They send out howls to communicate their locations, warn of other predators in the area, and discuss the position of prey. "In an open area—in a space without many hills—wolves can hear another wolf's howl for ten miles," Moore says. In the forest, the range is more like 6 miles.

All this to say, wolves howl a lot when they're hunting, and their howls can really carry. When they hunt later into the night because there's extra light from a full or unusually bright moon, it might give off the impression that wolves are howling specifically at the moon. But they aren't. They're just using the moon as a nightlight.

Wolves howl for more reasons than we'll ever know. They howl day and night. They even use howls to communicate among packs, usually as a warning, Moore says, "Like, hey, you just stepped into our territory, and we're asking you nicely to leave before we remove you." From body language to scent, wolves actually have many modes of communicating, but the most important form of communication is vocal, and the most popularly known is howling.

Scientists are still learning about wolf howls and yips, decoding them, trying to understand what everything means. "What we do know is that every wolf has its own voice," says Mech. That's right! Wolves use tone and inflection, just like us, and they can even change their voices based on their mood or with whom they're chatting. According to Moore, "Some scientists believe that the vocal communication system of wolves is as complex as the dolphin communication system."

BOTTOM LINE: You don't have to be afraid of big, bad wolves anymore, and you never really did. Even though wolves have stirred up some hot political debates by snatching livestock, the formidable canines are rarely dangerous to outdoors enthusiasts. There's no such thing as an alpha wolf, and contrary to popular belief, howling under a full moon only happens in clip art and bad memes.

Earthquakes 101

On August 17, 1959, in southwestern Montana, between Glacier National Park and Yellowstone, most of the campers at *Rock Creek* were already zipped into their tents at 11:37 p.m., when the ground began to clatter and sway. There was a crashing sound—louder than thunder—and then guests staying at nearby lodges heard the screams.

Measuring in at magnitude 7.3, the Hebgen Lake earthquake was the strongest and deadliest in Montana's history, setting off a massive landslide in Madison Canyon that sent 50 million cubic yards of rock, soil, mud, and debris down the south canyon wall at nearly 100 miles per hour, partly burying a recreational campground situated on the valley floor.

The quake caused 28 fatalities, with most recreationists perishing in landslides at Rock Creek and the nearby Cliff Lake Campground. Those who didn't die in the landslide were trapped in the canyon overnight by debris and damaged highways. As if that weren't awful enough, the tremor caused a seiche, that is, a temporary disturbance in the water level of Hebgen Lake. So survivors watched in horror as lake water sloshed around like crazy. A few big waves even breached the lake's dam, leading the victims to wonder if the dam was going to fail while they were still trapped inside the canyon.

It was a worst-nightmare scenario, to say the least, and the deadly event is a serious reminder that earthquakes can occur anytime, anywhere. Yet few outdoors enthusiasts bother to prepare for quakes and their aftershocks.

But wait, you say, I'm backpacking through Virginia's Blue Ridge Mountains, or hiking in Colorado's rugged backcountry, or camping inside Mark Twain National Forest in Missouri, and so earthquakes are the last thing on my mind because the big ones really only happen in California. That right there is the first earthquake fallacy we need to bust.

It's a myth that all major North American earthquakes occur in California.

While the Golden State has definitely seen its share of major seismic activity, "Earthquakes happen everywhere," says Alexandra Hatem, a research geologist at the US Geological Survey's Geologic Hazards Science Center. They're not just a California problem. In fact, Alaska registers the most earthquakes annually, with California placing second. Using the USGS's interactive earthquake catalog (available at earthquake.usgs.gov/earthquakes/search), users can search for seismic activity across the country, setting criteria based on region, time frame, or magnitude. Wyoming, Idaho, Utah, Nevada, Texas, and Oklahoma all recorded dozens of quakes in 2021.

Despite the facts, the myth remains that California is the earthquake capital of the United States. Hatem thinks this misguided notion can be traced back to the 1800s. "In 1857," she explains, "there was a very large earthquake in Southern California." With an estimated magnitude of 7.9, the Fort Tejon earthquake was—and still is—one of the most significant earthquakes in American history. (It was so colossal that it actually left a 225-mile scar along the fault trace where it originated.)

Relatively little is known about the seismic activity that contributed to the Fort Tejon earthquake. The scientific study of earthquakes is a newer field, after all, and until the 1700s, Earth scientists really weren't recording much quantitative information about earthquakes—although ancient cultures such as China and Japan have very long records of damaging earthquakes.

The Fort Tejon earthquake sent shocks from Parkfield down to the town of Wrightwood, and people just sort of assumed that Southern California must be a hotspot for tremors. "A lot of people moved to Northern California," says Hatem, both to escape what they thought was an earthquake zone and also to participate in the California Gold Rush.

Then 49 years later, the next major earthquake struck—this time in Northern California! Although the 1906 San Francisco earthquake lasted less than a minute, it wreaked havoc, killing an estimated 3,000 people, leaving half the city's residents homeless, and igniting fires that burned for days and destroyed nearly 500 city blocks.

"The 1906 San Francisco earthquake and the 1857 Fort Tejon earthquake are among the largest earthquakes we've had in the US since 1800," explains Hatem. It makes sense, then, that people assume California must be *the* place where major earthquakes transpire.

And here's the thing, behind the myth, there's also a nugget of truth. North America's West Coast really is more seismically active than the rest of the country. To understand why, we'll first need an in-depth rundown on earthquakes.

"Basically," Hatem says, "an earthquake is the rapid release of energy. That energy," she continues, "comes from two tectonic plates either coming together or bumping up next to each other."

Let's say you've got a sink filled with soapy dishwater, and there are a few rigid dinner plates floating about, bumping into each other while they're waiting to be cleaned. The dinner plates represent the world's tectonic plates, which are basically these giant, oddly shaped slabs of solid rock. "Scientists debate how many tectonic plates there are," Hatem says, noting that "there are ten or so major plates plus many smaller ones."

"When the edges of two plates meet, that area's called a plate boundary," Hatem continues. Plate boundaries contain a fault, and Hatem says, "Earthquakes occur primarily along these faults, when two plates collide." If one plate is slightly denser than the other, the heavy plate slips right underneath the lighter plate. And then, watch out: A major earthquake is coming.

Most earthquakes occur around the Pacific Ocean, which claims the world's greatest earthquake zone, the circum-Pacific seismic belt. Nicknamed the Ring of Fire, this is where 81 percent of the planet's largest earthquakes happen. The belt extends from Chile all the way up the West Coast and into the southern part of Alaska. From there it runs west to Japan, the Philippine Islands, New Guinea, the Southwest Pacific, and finally to New Zealand.

Hatem points out that "California sits right on a tectonic plate boundary," the San Andreas fault, which is the main boundary between the Pacific and North American plates. Southern California records about 10,000 earthquakes annually, and that's just a drop in the bucket considering there are approximately 500,000 detectable earthquakes in the world every year. According to the US Geological Survey's website, though, only about one-fifth of these yearly quakes can be felt, and a mere 100 cause damage.

"A lot of little earthquakes are happening all the time," Hatem reiterates. "Most are very small, something like magnitude 2 or 3," she adds.

Geologists measure earthquake size using something called magnitude, a marker that essentially describes the amount of energy a quake releases.

*A common misconception is that the magnitude scale
ends at 10.*

There's no upper limit, and yet Hatem says, "Some people
think the scale goes from 1 to 10. This is just not true."

For all intents and purposes, though, the scale might as
well end at 10, at least for the time being. The largest magnitude earthquake ever recorded was 9.5 in 1960 when the
Valdivia Earthquake leveled Chile's Pacific Rim. Following
that was the 1964 Great Alaska Earthquake, measuring in at
magnitude 9.2.

It's true that the West Coast has racked up some
high-magnitude quakes. But that certainly doesn't mean other
parts of the country are unaffected. "Less active doesn't mean
inactive," Hatem says. Two of the most significant seismic
events in American history happened in South Carolina
in 1886 and, before that, along the New Madrid Fault in
Missouri.

In the winter of 1811 and 1812, a seismic zone near
New Madrid, Missouri, produced a series of tremors that
lasted for several months, including three very large earthquakes estimated to be between magnitude 7 and 8. In
addition to destroying quite a few settlements along the
Mississippi River, the force of the land upheaval created two
temporary waterfalls on the Mississippi, and according to
accounts from boatmen, the Mississippi River ran backwards
for several hours.

Convulsions from the New Madrid Earthquakes caused
structural damage as far away as Cincinnati, and although the
events occurred in the central Mississippi Valley, they were felt
over a thousand miles away, in Washington, DC, New York
City, and Hartford, Connecticut. In his book *Travels in the
Interior of America in the Years 1809, 1810 and 1811*, naturalist
John Bradbury provided his eyewitness account of the aftershock from one of the New Madrid earthquakes:

I could distinctly see the river as if agitated by a storm;
and although the noise was inconceivably loud and terrific,
I could distinctly hear the crash of falling trees, and the
screaming of the wild fowl on the river, but found that the
boat was still safe at her moorings.

In case you're curious, Florida and North Dakota have the
fewest earthquakes each year. In the past hundred years, since
1921, Florida hasn't recorded a single quake above a magnitude 2.5, and North Dakota has had only four such tremors
(half of them occurred on the state's western border, practi-
cally in Montana). So if you're recreating in these locales, feel
free to ignore the following advice, but be sure to review "The
Supernatural Wonder We Call Lightning."

The truly bone-chilling thing about earthquakes is that, at
least for now, there's really no good, scientific way to predict
when one will happen. "We can't reliably predict what we can't
see," Hatem says. Since earthquakes begin miles—sometimes
hundreds of miles!—below the surface, scientists can't observe
seismic events as they form. While tools such as seismometers
are now available to track and evaluate an earthquake's waves,
these measurements can only be made as an earthquake is
actually happening—not before one occurs.

Although scientists can't reliably predict earthquakes,
people have long speculated that animals are capable of filling
in the gaps. Since the early medieval period—yes, we're talking
Before Common Era—there have been accounts of animals
displaying unusual behavior in anticipation of earthquakes.
And as recently as 2011, the *Washington Post* ran a story stating that several animals at the National Zoo in Washington,
DC, including Iris, an orangutan, predicted the 2011 Virginia
earthquake, a record-setting magnitude 5.8 event that sent
tremors up and down the East Coast on August 23.

Right before the earthquake rattled DC, Iris and other
National Zoo residents cried out then scrambled around

inside their enclosures, leading some observers to think they had instinctually predicted the forthcoming tremor.

These stories are really fun, but unfortunately it's a myth that animals can accurately predict earthquakes.
In reality, animals are probably just feeling something called the P wave, or primary wave, which is a preliminary (and less intense) wave preceding an earthquake's notable S wave. Secondary waves, along with other surface waves, are the waves that move the ground enough to do damage to the built environment.

Interestingly, scientists can quickly detect P waves, too, and the USGS uses sensor data to produce an early earthquake warning system called the ShakeAlert for millions of people on the West Coast. "This is not a prediction system," Hatem notes. By the time a ShakeAlert goes out, an earthquake is already well under way. Those who receive messages will have just a few extra moments to get to a safe place and drop and cover before the S wave appears. But when it comes to earthquake safety, even seconds can greatly improve outcomes.

Just like animals can't predict earthquakes, weather also seems to have very little bearing on tremors.

It's a myth, for example, that earthquakes are more common in dry, hot weather.

This misconception dates all the way back to the ancient Greeks. But today we know "there's no such thing as 'earthquake weather,'" Hatem says. Earthquakes start forming miles underground, and they can happen in any kind of weather. It is also pure lore that big earthquakes emerge at particular times of the day. And even though the moon does bring on tides that can potentially put stress on solid parts of the Earth, like plates, geophysicist Susan Hough concluded in 2018 that the time of day doesn't play any substantial role in seismic activity.

In her study, Hough took all earthquakes magnitude 8 and over from the 1600s to today and ran an analysis to see if there were any meaningful patterns in what time of year or at which point in the lunar cycle, they occurred. Do earthquakes have preferred days or times? According to the supremely brief, one-word abstract to her study, the answer is, "No."

We don't know when or where the next Big One will be. But on the bright side, Hatem says, "Scientists now have a fairly good understanding of aftershocks." The US Geological Survey, for example, has become really skilled at delivering reliable aftershock forecasting, which can help people remain safe through the smaller earthquakes that happen after an initial quake.

An earthquake itself isn't all that deadly, after all, and ground movement from the main quake is rarely what causes widespread injury and death. Most disaster movies produced over the last century portray earthquakes as these insane, apocalyptic events where fault lines literally open up wide enough to swallow people and buildings whole. That's not actually how it works when the camera isn't rolling.

Some people are under the mistaken impression that, during earthquakes, the ground opens wide. This is not what happens.

"Sometimes there are small fissures that can be a few feet deep," Hatem admits, but even that's relatively rare. During a quake, the ground moves *across* a fault, not away from it, and that's what creates the energy that causes the earthquake. If the fault opened, there'd be no friction and thus no tremor.

Even if the ground doesn't physically separate, earthquakes can still be horrifying natural disasters, especially if you're caught in one while recreating outdoors in unfamiliar terrain. There are quite a few tips, though, that can help keep you safe.

Most of the danger from earthquakes comes from falling debris or damage to infrastructure. In the wilderness, it's easy to avoid buildings, but there are still other things that can come crashing down. Try to get to an open area, where trees, rocks, and power lines can't fall on you.

If possible, Hatem says, "Get to a safe and sturdy place, away from windows and glass that could break." Then drop onto your hands and knees, use one arm and hand to cover your head and neck, and hold on until the shaking stops. Don't return to heavily constructed spots too soon after tremors stop. The most dangerous place to be during an earthquake and its aftershocks is near building exteriors, but even that nice, shady tree you pitched your tent under becomes a potential threat since some trees lose branches during seismic shaking, while others snap and fall down entirely.

Keep an eye out for potential dangers, but don't rush to the nearest building. If you're caught outdoors, it's best to simply stay put.

It's a myth that the safest place to be in an earthquake is in a doorframe.

"That's outdated advice," explains Hatem, noting, "That advice actually comes from an earthquake that happened in 1872 in Owens Valley, California." Back then, people were still building their homes out of mud and adobe, and in these unreinforced masonry structures, sometimes the only thing left standing after an earthquake was the wooden doorframe. Observers figured that the doorframe must be the safest place to stand. Nowadays, though, if you're indoors, it's always best to seek shelter underneath a sturdy table. Doorframes today usually have doors that can swing open and injure you.

If you're camping when an earthquake strikes, get out of your tent immediately. There's a chance the canvas might get tangled up and suffocate you. Also, if a campfire was burning before the quake, move away from the flame, and then put the fire out completely (see "Do Campfires Serve a Purpose?") as soon as it's safe to do so.

With really large-scale disasters, like earthquakes, emergency responders might need some extra time to respond, especially if there's road damage leading to your campground, picnic site, or the trailhead where you parked. Campers and RVers who are truly prepared for anything will have enough extra supplies to take care of themselves for days, if necessary.

Could you "dry camp" for at least three days, without any external source of water? In addition to extra water, get into the habit of packing extra food, too, as well as a first aid kit, batteries, and personal hygiene items, plus any prescription medications you'd need for at least a few additional days. If you're adventuring with pets, don't forget about their food and water needs, too.

Lastly, if you were recreating near the shore, the best advice is to immediately evacuate to higher ground, even if the shaking lasts only for a few seconds. According to the National Oceanic and Atmospheric Administration, tsunamis are most commonly generated by an earthquake where there's a sudden displacement of the ocean floor.

Don't wait to see if a wall of water comes to shore, and don't wait for officials to sound the warning alarm, either. As quickly as possible, move inland at least 2 miles, or climb to land that is at least 100 feet above sea level. It's best to walk quickly as drivers could run into traffic or debris on the road.

When it comes to earthquakes, there are some real risks to worry about, and there's every reason to be prepared. But you don't need to fear a future filled with a never-ending stream of back-to-back tremors.

It's a myth that earthquakes are becoming more frequent.

Seismologists might not be able to reliably predict earthquakes yet, but due to technological advancements, they're able to monitor and measure them. As seismological centers have cropped up across the country, and scientists have been able to use new instruments to locate smaller, previously immeasurable tremors, it can sometimes appear that more earthquakes are happening more often. But actually, Hatem says, "Research shows that earthquakes of magnitude 7.0 or greater remained constant throughout the century and have actually started decreasing in recent years."

And climate change shouldn't have a sizeable impact on earthquakes either. "Plate tectonics will happen with or without climate change," Hatem explains. That said, she adds, "Things like increased flooding could trigger earthquakes if the scenario is right." Climate change also creates an increased risk of aftereffects such as tsunamis in vulnerable coastal areas.

BOTTOM LINE: Earthquakes aren't just a West Coast occurrence. They can happen anytime, anywhere, and even though scientists can't reliably predict when they'll strike, all outdoors enthusiasts have the power to be prepared for tremors when recreating outside.

Do Campfires Serve a Purpose?

The sun dips below the horizon like a brilliant orange orb. As the fleeting colors of dusk fade into black, your three-season tent rustles in a frigid October wind. The cold's hardly a concern, though, because you're already stationed 'round a campfire with your group, drinking a craft beer, glad for the heat the fire generates on a crisp fall night in the backcountry.

Circling the fire pit, telling yarns into the wee hours, "This is the quintessential wilderness experience," says Andrew Terrill, an outdoors enthusiast and author of *The Earth Beneath My Feet* and *On Sacred Ground*.

But are all those roaring flames really doing anything to keep you warm or safe from nocturnal predators? Campfires have been the subject of some—ahem—*heated* debate among outdoorsy circles. According to Terrill, fires are "purely a cultural thing." As he puts it, "You end up losing body heat while standing outside around a fire."

Wilderness EMT and all-around outdoors expert Erik Kulick agrees. He runs a series of multiday field courses out of the True North Wilderness Survival School in Pennsylvania, and at the outset of every class Kulick asks his students to list their top priorities in a survival situation. "The first two things mentioned are almost always food and fire," he says.

Quite simply, food is not a priority. Sure, many of the preppers on YouTube start rummaging for sustenance the minute the camera's rolling. "That's all for show," Kulick says. Logically, it wouldn't make any sense to prioritize food since, as Kulick notes, "Although you may feel hungry and a bit weak after a couple of days without having eaten, you can still function. You've got thirty-plus days before you'll begin to starve."

You don't need a fire to cook the squirrel you've just trapped because you aren't wasting time hunting for food—not on your first nights lost, anyway. But will glowing flames provide warmth and protection?

Campfires aren't your best bet for warmth, but they can be useful for other things such as signaling for help.

When you really stop to think about it, "prioritizing a fire doesn't make much sense, either," according to Kulick. For most people, in most situations, fires take a whole lot of energy and effort to build. To start one from scratch, the first step is the arduous, time-consuming process of collecting wood, and if it's cold, damp, or windy, well, then you're traipsing around in some pretty undesirable conditions, all with the end game of eventually, maybe, becoming warm.

Even if the elements aren't so bad, time will probably be working against you. "Most people don't decide they're lost until late in the day, when the sun's already low in the sky," explains Kulick. By then, there might not be enough sunlight left for gathering a sufficient amount of wood.

For the sake of argument, let's say you end up lost right next to a perfect pile of dry wood. How were you planning to start your fire? Most of Kulick's students want to learn to make a fire the old-fashioned way, using a friction method. "I know the guys on television make it look easy, but making a fire with friction isn't easy," Kulick says.

"Making a friction fire off the land—gathering wood, building a bow drill kit—is a highly technical skill that takes lots of practice," adds Nathan Summers, author of *Awakening Fire: The Essential Guide to Flame, Wood, and Ignition.*

Bushcraft can be a fun skill to learn, but in a real-life survival situation, you shouldn't rely on antiquated techniques. If something is actually wrong, always opt for the easy, modern method. When it comes to fire making, plan to use contemporary tools, including matches or a lighter and tinder, which are listed as important survival items on The 10 Essentials, a comprehensive packing list for every type of outdoor adventurer.

"Carry at least one, possibly two, sources of ignition in your pack," Summers says, recommending that all outdoors enthusiasts travel with waterproof matches and a lighter. Remember, too, that matches have a shelf life, so make a mental note now to restock your pack once every few months.

Wood fuels fires, and contrary to popular belief, it is usually possible to burn damp wood.

"Once you get a good fire going, wet wood will burn," Summers says. Soggy wood produces more smoke than dry wood. When you're camping, smoke is a bad thing. If you're lost in the wilderness, though, Summers argues that it's beneficial since both the physical vapor and scent from a fire can signal to potential rescuers where you are.

While fire provides continual warmth throughout the day and night, Kulick says most people would be better off focusing on shelter. Gathering wood can be a major time suck, after all, and once you get your fire going, "you are only warming half of your body at a time, and you're still out there in the elements, exposed to wind, possibly being rained on," says Kulick.

Science backs up this assertion. "There are several ways heat moves around," explains geoscientist Elizabeth Gordon, professor and chair of Earth and Geographic Sciences at

Fitchburg State University. All matter is made up of molecules and atoms that are in constant motion. The motion creates something called thermal energy that we humans feel as heat. Thermal energy travels from one place to another in three ways: radiation, convection, and conduction.

The blazing-hot sun, for example, transmits its light and warmth through empty space by direct radiation, which travels as electromagnetic waves, Gordon explains. A campfire isn't nearly as warm as the sun, yet it still gives off radiation. "You have to be really close to a campfire to get radiant energy from it," Gordon says, adding that "most of the fire's heat rises into the atmosphere, and the energy is lost through a process called convection."

Even though Kulick describes fire as "a quintessential part of survival training," he really doesn't emphasize it the way other instructors might. "What I focus on in my classes is making shelter," Kulick explains. "If I needed to stay warm, I'd rather take my limited resources and build something that I can curl up inside of."

Gordon confirms that scientifically speaking, it's best to be holed up inside a small shelter. "Your body heat warms the air inside the tent, and then the tent itself prevents the exchange of your body's heat with the cold air outside," she explains. Convection is happening inside your shelter, but now it is working to your advantage!

Kulick's the first to admit that The 10 Essentials can be overkill. Extra food, for example, isn't absolutely essential for short-term survival, and while it's a great thing to slather on when recreating outdoors on a sunny day, sunscreen won't keep you alive in the woods overnight.

A lightweight tarp or bivy, though, really is an essential item. "It's possibly the number one piece of survival gear," says Summers. According to Kulick, everyone should carry some type of waterproof, windproof sheeting in their daypack, regardless of how long they're planning to be outdoors.

Space blankets (sometimes called Mylar blankets) are popular among outdoors enthusiasts and survivalists. While these NASA-designed, metal-coated sheets are literally made to retain heat, Kulick says, "They're too small, for one, and they rip easily."

The ideal size sheeting is at least 10 feet by 10 feet, or 100 square feet. Kulick recommends buying a 2-mil roll of plastic drop cloth from the local hardware store. It's not fancy, but it doesn't have to be. In addition to being windproof, waterproof, and pliable, a plastic drop cloth is also thick enough to make a rugged shelter large enough to hold three to four people. Best of all, a packaged roll fits easily into most kits and packs and will only set you back about $4.50.

Armed with the right drop cloth, you'll be able to make a rudimentary shelter in as little as 30 seconds. "Unfurl the material, wrap it around yourself, and you're protected from the rain and wind," Kulick says. If you are also carrying string, rope, or a parachute cord, you can easily make a lean-to in 30 minutes or less, by tying one side of your sheeting to a tree and using rocks or brush to tether the other end to the earth.

If you get lost, and you've failed to pack these items, Kulick says, "You are likely limited to the stereotypical debris shelter—sticks and leaves—which can take several hours to make windproof and waterproof." In this case, he adds, "Prior preparation and practice is paramount." If you get lost in the wilderness, and you can't build a shelter, Summers says, "The best idea would be to utilize a natural shelter, such as a tree or rock, and then build a fire in front of you." And where you choose to build a shelter can be every bit as important as the materials you use.

It's a myth that you'll find the warmest campsite down on the valley floor.

While ridges tend to be windier than valleys, a draw, which is the low ground between two steep-sided ridges, can collect something called katabatic air, which gets very cold at night. "All low areas, particularly valleys near water, tend to be cooler," Kulick says, likening the phenomenon to an air-conditioned home. As the night turns cool, warmer air rises, and cold air flows in to take its place.

While a cool night's breeze might offer welcome relief in the summer, if it's winter and you're already cold, Kulick says, "Setting up camp in a low area might not be the best idea." But don't rush up to the top of a ridge, either. Ridges tend to be windier, chillier places.

According to Kulick, "The overriding rule is to find a place that's safe." When he's setting up camp for a night outdoors, Kulick avoids so-called widow-makers, which he describes as, "anything that might fall down and kill you in your sleep."

Whether you're lost and looking for a place to build a shelter, or you're camping in the backcountry and need to set up your campsite, start by finding relatively flat terrain. Next, stretch out your arms, and turn around in a circle, Kulick says. As you make a 360-degree revolution, look for anything hazardous, especially cliffs. Now put your arm up at a 45-degree angle and take another spin. Is there a tree that might collapse, or branches that could fall? "Even in local and state parks, people die every year on relatively tame campouts," Kulick says.

Once you've found the right spot, curl up inside your tarp, and hopefully in the morning you'll be well rested enough to make some good decisions that will get you out of the woods safely. And if you hear something go bump in the night, try not to reconsider your stance on fires.

Campfires haven't been proven or disproven to scare away predators and other animals.

According to Summers, "It is well understood that smoke in general will repel animals." Fire, after all, is inherently dangerous to wildlife and has been since early humans first discovered fire. Other experts argue that the presence of humans sitting around a fire is what deters most big mammals, including wolves, coyotes, cougars, and bears. As Kulick puts it, "With wildlife, we are the most frightening aspect of the campfire."

Both lines of thinking make sense, and the jury's still out on whether campfires play a role in scaring off wild animals. "I don't know of anyone who could provide a definitive answer to this question," says wildlife biologist Brian Dreher, the terrestrial section manager for Colorado Parks and Wildlife. "It would require some experimentation to know for sure, and I am not aware of anyone ever looking into this," Dreher continues.

But anecdotally he adds, "It serves to reason that [fire] would help to keep large animals away." Teasing apart the impact of the fire and the impact of humans as a deterrent, though, would be a difficult task.

In the frontcountry—specifically campgrounds in state and regional parks—it's worth noting that certain animals, including bears and raccoons, are sometimes drawn *toward* a campfire when people are using the flames to cook their food.

Kulick doesn't think fire is an effective method for warming a human body or warding off predators and pests. But here's the thing: "Campfires are primal, and they're really fun to build," he says. According to Kulick, a fire's main value is psychological. If you're trying to survive, the biggest benefit you'll get from fire is an emotional boost.

"Fires make people feel safe because they can see their surroundings," says Ben Lawhon, senior director of research and consulting for the Leave No Trace Center for Outdoor Ethics. "As soon as you take light away, now you hear all the creepy crawlies, and you're scared," adds Kulick. Psychology can't be overlooked. In a true survival situation, emotional stability can be the difference between life and death. "Attitude," Kulick explains, "is the most important factor contributing to positive outcomes." If a fire makes you feel good, go ahead and make one, and don't feel guilty about the impact, either.

It's a myth that campfires contradict Leave No Trace principles.

Of course, not everyone who goes out into the woods will get lost. For many campers and RVers, campfires are a meaningful part of the outdoors experience. "There are lots of people who can't fathom camping without a fire," Lawhon says. And the good news is it's totally possible to enjoy a campfire while also being a great steward of the environment.

"Leave No Trace is not and fire. That's a big misconception," Lawhon says, clarifying, "We are pro-responsible fire." When done right, Lawhon continues, fires can really add to the outdoors experience, and Leave No Trace offers guidance for those who want to burn a campfire that leaves little impact on the local environment.

"The majority of US wildfires are caused by humans, through carelessness or arson," Lawhon explains, pointing to statistics generated by the National Interagency Fire Center, an Idaho-based organization of national fire management programs for the Bureau of Indian Affairs, Bureau of Land Management, US Fish and Wildlife Service, National Park Service, and the USDA Forest Service, along with other partners.

While the numbers are always in flux, Lawhon says the most current figures show that there were 73,110 wildfires on national forest lands between 2006 and 2015. "Almost half of those were caused by people," Lawhon says. In fact, campfires accounted for about one-third of human-caused fires, and those 24,370 blazes burned over 1.2 million acres of land. "To put it into perspective, that's like burning half of Yellowstone National Park," adds Lawhon.

"Across the country, around 80 percent of wildfires are caused by humans," Lawhon continues, and they cost taxpayers a small fortune to mitigate. In federal fiscal year 2017, for example, the total cost of putting out fires was $2.9 billion across the five federal land management agencies. "There's a huge financial cost to wildfire, and a lot of it is avoidable," Lawhon reiterates.

Assuming you're in an area where fires are allowed (be sure to check your site's rules ahead of time) you'll need to ask yourself, "Is it safe to build a fire tonight?" If it's windy, or overly dry, then you might have to forgo the flames.

Once you've determined that conditions are favorable for a campfire, the next question to ask is, "Do I have the skills to build a fire . . . and put it out properly?" This might seem counterintuitive, but let's start with the end in mind.

Putting out a campfire means putting it out cold. "We're talking cold to the touch," Lawhon says.

Contrary to popular belief, it's not a good idea to use soil or sand to smother flames.

"Smothering a fire doesn't always extinguish it," explains Lawhon. Under Leave No Trace guidelines, campers should use "copious amounts of water," as Lawhon puts it, to extinguish their fire. We're talking enough H_2O to make a pool in the fire pit, and then you're going to take a shovel or long stick and swirl all the coal, ash, and burnt logs around. Just be careful of steam as you stir.

While it's best to burn all wood to ash, if any pieces remain, turn them over so you're getting every side wet. "You want the debris to be cold to the point where you can run your hand through the ashes," says Lawhon. That's how you know your fire is out.

When campers fail to fully extinguish a fire, and then the wind picks up, that's exactly how some massive wildfires get going. You can't stop lightning from igniting a forest fire, but you can ensure your campfire doesn't spark one.

Assuming you have the wherewithal to properly put out your fire, now you're ready to build one. First Lawhon says, "Look for an existing ring." This isn't just a frontcountry request: Even in the backcountry, there may be a preexisting rock-rimmed ring to leverage. "If it's there, use it," Lawhon says, explaining that by using an existing ring campers can minimize ground disturbance and the ecological impact of gathering and blackening new rocks.

All you A+ students can earn extra credit by carrying a fire pan, which is a metal device resembling an upside down trash can lid. Fire pans can be suspended on rocks for zero-trace fires, and they're so effective they're often required items for recreationists traveling along river corridors.

Fire requires three basic things: oxygen, ignition, and fuel. Mother Nature supplies the oxygen, but you can help facilitate the natural process by building a fire structure that allows oxygen to flow easily. Summers is partial to A-frames and teepees and discusses all the options in his book, *Awakening Fire*.

It's up to you to figure out the remaining elements of heat and fuel. To get a fire going, you'll need tinder, that is, small amounts of brittle material such as dry grass/leaves or bark. You're looking for "something light and fluffy to start your fire," as Summers puts it, adding, "You'll need kindling, too, which is pencil-sized wood."

Whether you're using a pan or a ring, skip the giant logs whenever possible. Instead, build your campfire with small, brittle twigs that snap when you bend them and a commercial fire-starter (if available). Then add slightly bigger branches into the mix. From a Leave No Trace standpoint, Lawhon says, "It's best to build fires with wood no larger than your wrist that you find on the ground." This way you can leave a "clean ring" by burning your wood to ash. To ensure you'll be able to put your fire out cold, stop feeding the fire an hour or so before you plan to hunker down.

In some campgrounds, it's illegal to gather firewood. Check local rules prior to your outing, and if collecting wood is prohibited, purchase wood in the area where you're going to burn it. As a very general rule of thumb, 50 miles is too far, and 10 miles or less is best. "This practice prevents campers from transporting invasive weeds, as well as insects and diseases," Lawhon explains. If gathering firewood is allowed at your site, pick up dead and downed lumber off the ground.

For the sake of your health, avoid burning anything other than wood. Researchers at the Missoula Technology and Development Center completed a fascinating study in 2004 that looked at toxins released from burning various types of trash that campers commonly toss into their fires.

The scientists studied everything from paper plates to old batteries—yes, there are people who burn batteries—and discovered that campers who burn trash breathe in carcinogens while kicking back around the fire. "Don't ever burn toilet paper," Lawhon adds, noting that TP has been linked to an exorbitant number of human-caused wildfires. "All that should really go into a fire is wood," Lawhon reiterates, plain and simple.

No matter how careful you are, it's worth noting that even very responsible campers likely impact the local environment with their fires. "Fires give off particulates and carbon dioxide," explains Gordon. "One single campfire isn't horrendous," she says, "but scaling can be problematic."

If you have a bunch of different groups burning campfires daily over the course of a summer in a small geographic region, well, Gordon says, "That could potentially influence air pollution in a negative way." But Gordon is quick to point out that many factors drive air quality, from a location's topography to weather patterns. "There are so many variables," says Gordon. So if you love having a campfire, build one the Leave No Trace way.

"Fire is our campground TV," Lawhon notes. Historically, he says, "People used fire for light, warmth, and cooking. Now we have all these modern alternatives, but that doesn't mean we can't still enjoy a fire responsibly."

BOTTOM LINE: Whether you're recreating in the front- or backcountry, campfires are a fun activity. They're safe if you follow basic Leave No Trace guidelines. If you're actually lost in the woods, though, trying to survive, then you need to re-think your emotional attachment to the flame. Depending on the situation and weather conditions, you might be better off using your limited time and energy to make a shelter that you can crawl into for continued warmth.

The Fairy-Tale Life of Moss

Annie Martin's 2,000-square-foot moss garden really comes to life after a downpour, when dewdrops encapsulate zillions of thin, upright sporophytes. In these moments, the moss's reproductive structures look like "little, glimmering jewels," Martin says, floating in a rolling sea of dense green matting containing a range of complex hues, from Granny Smith apple to olive, jade, and even aquamarine.

The glow is more pronounced at night, under the moonlight. That's because, Martin explains in her thick drawl, "Mosses have leaves that are typically only one cell layer thick." Hence, this unique plant transmits light rather than absorbing it.

A moss garden is the perfect place to dance under a canopy of stars or howl at the moon (see "Wolves, Explained"). Although many people associate moss with serenity, Martin fancies her garden as a place for celebration. You don't have to be particularly calm to hear moss whisper its timeless wisdom. And you don't have to be an experienced botanist to partake in the scientific study of mosses.

To the naked, untrained eye, all mosses look kind of similar: "Smooth, green, small, and compact," says bryologist Matt von Konrat, PhD, head of botanical collections at the Field Museum in Chicago. But there's more to moss than meets the eye, and plenty of reasons to take a closer look. You won't need a true microscope: A measly hand lens that fits into your daypack is powerful enough to reveal the remarkable diversity among the world's 20,000-plus bryophytes, a group of plants that includes mosses, liverworts, and hornworts.

"Liverworts can often resemble mosses, but have a top-bottom orientation, whereas mosses have little top-bottom distinction," explains bryologist Janice Glime, PhD, professor emerita at Michigan Technological University. Hornworts, meanwhile, have a bladelike thallus, and the sporophyte resembles a horn. "All are small," adds Glime, and the origin of all three groups is ancient. Hold onto your hand lens because this next bit is truly mind-boggling: Mosses are believed to be ancestors of every green plant we see today.

Beyond their cushiony softness, "Mosses have tremendous visual appeal," Martin writes in her book, *The Magical World of Moss Gardening.* The plant really is magical, offering texture and depth to any garden, plus color galore. "While green may dominate a moss landscape," Martin notes, "you can expect brilliant jewel-tone colors—crimson red, pale pink, tangerine orange, and sunshine yellow."

"Mosses have this really unique feel," Martin continues, and it's best to be barehanded when working them so you can really appreciate the tactile experience. Depending on the species, Martin says, "Some mosses are very soft, and some have a density to them that I feel as firmness." All mosses are tiny, typically 1 to 10 centimeters tall, though some are only microscopic in size, and they're herbaceous (i.e., non-woody). "Every single colony you see is composed of hundreds of thousands, if not millions, of individual plants," Martin says, adding, that thing that looks like a leaf to you is actually the entire plant—a bunch of individuals within the mass.

When she isn't running her landscaping business, Mountain Moss Enterprises, Martin spends a good chunk of her time rescuing mosses because, she says, "The magic of mosses can touch your heart and your spirit all year long." Unlike other green plants, mosses don't die back in the cold. "In fact, they thrive," Martin says, revealing that mosses can—and frequently will!—have sex underneath a blanket of snow.

For outdoors enthusiasts Martin says, "Mosses are going to jump at you in the wintertime because everything else besides evergreens will be dead or dormant." But while mosses are often associated with the woods, these resilient, low-maintenance plants can literally grow anywhere, including between the cracks of city sidewalks.

"Mosses occur on every continent and in every location that's habitable by photosynthetic plants," says Glime. As Martin puts it, "There is something magical in plants that can live in such dramatically different environmental conditions."

Since childhood, Martin has connected with mosses, and that's a fitting time for any moss infatuation to begin: Small and mysterious, mosses grow under the canopy of old growth forests, conjuring up childish images of elves, trolls, and dwarves. "Moss is a fairy-tale plant, a whole miniature world, a tiny forest for microbes and insects," says von Konrat.

If a field of moss evokes images of a fairy-tale castle and "once upon a time," it might be because this ancient species grew in the shadows of medieval castles and has literally been around since once upon a time. Mosses are 450 million years old. "They have watched every cataclysmic disaster occur on this planet, and they're still here," Martin points out.

Every species of moss is unique, and yet all mosses share a few important commonalities. They're plants, so they produce chlorophyll, which means they harvest sunlight and carbon dioxide to create their own food through the process of photosynthesis. But unlike some flowering plants, "Most mosses don't have to have direct sunlight," Glime clarifies. There are plenty of mosses and liverworts that live in cracks in caves, for example, and there's one liverwort, ghostwort, that doesn't have any chlorophyll at all but gets its nutrition through a relationship with a partner fungus.

Mosses absorb water and nutrients through their leaves and grow especially well on certain substrates such as soil, bark, and rock, though von Konrat points out that "different species are adapted to different habitats." In fact, choice of substrate varies by species, and some mosses are found on roofs or in the cracks of city sidewalks.

There's a common tip shared as outdoor knowledge that moss grows on the north side of trees, rocks, and buildings. That trick might help you out sometimes. But it'll steer you wrong just as often.

It's pure fiction that moss always grows on the north side of the tree.

Mosses couldn't give two hoots about the four cardinal directions of north, east, south, and west. "Moss grows where water gathers," says von Konrat. "Moisture and shade," he continues, "are key elements for the plant's survival."

It's almost that simple, and we could almost end the chapter right here. But there are exceptions to every rule. Some desert mosses, for example, can survive in sunny, arid habitats, though, generally speaking, most mosses need ample water to thrive. That's all due to the ancient plant's biology.

Remember learning about your body's circulatory system back in elementary school? Your teacher probably pulled out a laminated, anatomical poster cluttered head-to-toe with red and blue lines weaving around a human body, depicting a complex vascular system that delivers oxygen and nutrients to tissues inside our mortal bodies.

Vascular plants have remarkably similar systems. They suck up nutrients and water from the soil through their roots. Since photosynthesis occurs in the leaves, vascular plants then need to pump subsurface nourishment up through their stems and into their aboveground parts. Their vascular systems support the process.

It's a myth that all mosses are nonvascular plants.

Oftentimes botanists will classify mosses as "nonvascular plants," and they use this imprecise distinction to separate mosses from other green and flowering species within the kingdom. "This is a broadly touted misconception," Glime says, explaining that "mosses often do have vascular tissue."

Like so-called vascular plants, mosses are able to transport moisture throughout their teeny bodies. They aren't particularly efficient at carrying out the process, though, and at some point in time, they caught a rap for being nonvascular.

"Some of the transport is just cell-to-cell," Glime continues, "But many mosses have specialized cells in the stem and costa (leaf rib) that are elongated to provide more directed and faster transport." In fact, Glime says, "In some species, such as the haircap mosses, the structure is remarkably similar to the xylem and phloem in plants with lignified vascular tissue."

If you aren't a bryologist, that last sentence might have seemed complicated. All you really need to know is that many mosses have a harder time moving nutrients around because they lack lignin, which is a special material with really big molecules that's found in the walls of certain types of cells. Picture a tree. Lignin is the chemical that makes wood tough and hard. (Did you know wood itself is vascular tissue?)

Mosses also lack roots, meaning they have to absorb fluids and food through their leaves. This tidbit can be confusing for some observers because mosses have rhizoids, which sometimes resemble roots. Rhizoids are not roots, and in most cases, moss rhizoids serve only to attach a moss to its substrate. "Most bryophytes rely on cellular uptake from the surroundings at every location of the plant," Glime says. "Even mosses with good conducting systems can take up water through leaf cells," she adds.

Although mosses are sometimes confused with molds, which also thrive in wet, damp conditions, they are completely distinct organisms categorized in two entirely different biological ranks. Mold can grow green—true—but it's a member of the kingdom fungi, whereas mosses belong to the plant kingdom.

For the sake of survival, all moss cells need easy access to water straight from the environment. That's one of the reasons many mosses like hanging out in soggy places. Mosses also need moisture to reproduce, and this next part is what really fascinates many experts. Most flowering green plants reproduce sexually, through the processes of self-pollination and cross-pollination, both of which depend on the movement of seeds. Mosses, on the other hand, reproduce by spores, just like ferns and mushrooms (see "The Fungus among Us").

"Mosses have a really interesting reproduction life cycle," von Konrat begins. The males produce mobile sperm that scientists can see under a microscope. Just like human sperm, moss sperm needs a film of moisture to swim to an egg. "Even with desert moss, at some point in the year there will be some moisture, and that's when reproduction happens," says von Konrat. These unique physiological needs explain why mosses are so commonly observed on rocks near streambeds, creeks, river banks, and high mountain forests where there's lots of cloud cover.

It's easy to see why North Americans came to believe that mosses grow on the north side of things. In the tropics, rays from the sun hit the Earth's surface at a near-perpendicular angle. But because of the way Earth tilts on its axis, as you move away from the equator, the sun's rays will actually strike down at an angle. That explains why—in the Northern Hemisphere, at least—rooms with south-facing windows are typically brighter than those facing north.

This concept is critical to understanding moss because the north sides of objects in the Northern Hemisphere are naturally going to be shadier and cooler. Since water evaporates more slowly in shade, the north sides of trees and rocks will usually be damper and remain moist longer than the south sides of those same objects, where water evaporates quickly and life's quite a bit drier. North sides of things, then, are predisposed to having the damp surfaces most mosses need to carry out their vital functions. But that's thanks to the moisture, not the direction itself.

Whether or not moss primarily grows on the north side depends a lot on where you live. "While there's a tendency for moss to grow on the northern side of a tree in the Northern Hemisphere, if you're talking to someone Down Under, it's the complete opposite," von Konrat points out. (In the Southern Hemisphere, mosses have a tendency to grow on the south side for the same reasons.)

While it's a myth that mosses always grow on the north side, in the Northern Hemisphere it's fair to claim that mosses *often* grow on the north side. "Moss grows well on the north side, but it's certainly not restricted to that area," von Konrat summarizes. Everything from wind direction to a tree's natural slant can create the conditions moss prefers. "A lot depends on the forest itself," Glime says.

Take a hurricane zone, for example. Hurricanes can come in from the north, Glime explains, and strong winds can force moss onto the south side of objects, even in the Northern Hemisphere.

One of Glime's graduate students recently did a study on mosses growing in the Upper Peninsula of Michigan, a forested region notorious for its long, snowy winters. "He found that Upper Peninsula mosses were dominant on the south sides of trees. I'm guessing the reason is because our winds come from the north and northwest," says Glime, adding, "It is also likely that bryophytes can grow in the humid space between the snow and the tree trunk where the sun provides some melting and sufficient light through the snow."

Confused yet? Well, take a deep breath, because topography and climate are factors we have to consider, too. "In very flat terrain, it might be more common to see moss trending north," says von Konrat. But imagine if you're recreating in a hilly region, or you're deep in a valley where it's very shady. In these particular zones, von Konrat continues, "You'll often find bryophytes growing all around the tree." The old dad joke is that moss always grows on the outside of the tree, and that might be the safest rule of thumb (but also pretty useless).

It's a common misunderstanding that mosses only grow in moist environments.

Like any other living organism, mosses are diverse. "They can grow in a wide variety of habitats," von Konrat reiterates. "Most people think mosses grow in damp places, which is true, but lots also grow in very dry places," Glime says. Species such as *Fissidens grandifrons* grow in torrential waters of mountain streams and waterfalls; *Syntrichia inermis*, meanwhile, exist in arid, desert-like conditions.

Mosses have an incredible ability to recover from long periods of drying out. "They have much greater fortitude in drought than do most flowering plants," says Glime. As long as they dry slowly, mosses are able to prepare physiologically for drought. "Then, when they are moist, they are able to get up and running rather quickly to build new cell membranes or repair damaged ones and to begin photosynthesis," Glime continues. Bryophytes also respond crazy-fast to bursts of light. Since their leaves, in most species, are only one cell thick, photosynthesis can begin in seconds when sun flecks reach them.

While navigating with moss might just work in some environments and instances, this natural aid certainly doesn't replace a compass and a map.

For all the reasons outlined above, Glime says, "If you really know your area, if you're familiar with the forest, then you could possibly rely on moss as one tool for natural navigation." And for thousands of years, explorers really did use moss to navigate, along with the night sky (see "What's the North Star Good for Anyway?") and prevailing winds. For moss navigation to work, though, you'd need to be in an open, homogenous forest where the sun really did hit the trees from the south, and there were no complicating factors messing with how water gathers.

"Natural navigation tactics are only appropriate if you really know what you're doing," says survival expert Erik Kulick, a Wilderness EMT and founder of the True North Wilderness Survival School. When Kulick puts on his field instructor hat at True North, one of his main prerogatives is to train students to stay alive if they end up in a legit survival situation.

While the rationales behind the moss-north trick sound logical, Kulick says, "The big problem is that moss isn't genuinely reliable since there are so many factors that can influence how and where moss grows." If you're ever forced to trust your acumen and natural surroundings to avoid death, you really need to be employing tactics that are 100 percent accurate.

"If I'm looking for a navigation aid, there are other things I'd prefer to use," continues Kulick. "A lot of snow will remain on the north side of trees in winter, and I can quickly and repeatedly survey the area around me to confirm that it's consistent," he says. If you're a plant person who really knows their stuff—and you end up lost in the exact right region—then you might also be able to use *Silphium laciniatum*, the compass plant. Native to North America, and found in the eastern and central United States as far west as New Mexico, this plant's leaves are like a compass because they point from north to south.

Speaking of compasses, why not just carry a real compass along with a map? Take a land navigation course, too, then continue to practice when you're recreating outdoors. Kulick wears a thumb compass on his watchband so he can periodically check it as a quick and easy reference for staying oriented, and he uses a topographical map app for additional reference.

Kulick's a pro, though, and navigation is a technical skill that can take years to master. So even if you can figure out which way is north, is that information going to help you? "The reason you're using any of these methods is you're looking to orient yourself," Kulick says. And orientation is only useful if you're reasonably knowledgeable of your surroundings.

What if you lose your way while mountain biking during a vacation, in a forest you've never visited? When you have absolutely no idea where you are, knowing which way is north probably won't be enough to get you un-lost, Kulick points out. If you're actually lost, you probably won't know whether you need to walk north or south.

The truth is, even among outdoorsy crowds, "Most people don't know how to navigate," Kulick says, adding, "They don't know how to use a map, and they don't look at their surroundings while they're hiking."

Being lost isn't just a physical problem. "It's a psychological problem, too," Kulick continues. The mental reaction most people have to being lost in the wilderness is the same response mechanism you'd have if you were drowning in the ocean. People panic, and that's when they start making really bad decisions.

So if you're recreating outdoors, and you suddenly realize you're lost, S-T-O-P. This handy acronym has four components. First, **Stop**. Sit down and assess the situation. If you're really rattled, try taking some deep breaths until you feel calm enough to **Think**. Take time to reflect on what you'll need to do to survive. Now it's time to **Observe** the terrain and look for any familiar landmarks. Don't wait until it starts getting dark to **Plan** your next course of action.

There are seven main priorities in any emergency survival situation. In order of importance, they are: STOP (outlined above), provide first aid, seek shelter, build a fire, signal for help, drink water, and don't worry about food.

"Food is always the last priority," Kulick reiterates. Focus instead on PMA, or positive mental attitude, which is hands-down the most important thing you need to survive an unplanned stint in the wilderness. "If you panic and do something stupid, then it really doesn't matter whether you have shelter or signaling. Your situation will get worse," Kulick explains. First and foremost, he says, "Calm yourself down, and make sound decisions."

Even if moss can't be used reliably for natural navigation, this cool plant does have some other noteworthy applications. "Moss are good accumulators of heavy metals," says Glime. Because they're so small, they respond rapidly to changes in the environment. Hence, scientists can use moss to monitor air and water quality and evaluate pollution in the atmosphere.

But moss's most famous use was during WWI, when field nurses wrapped soldiers' wounds in peat moss, nature's bandage, complete with absorbent and antiseptic properties. "Mosses and liverworts have some really interesting biological activity against microbes, and in some cultures, they still have important medicinal significance," says von Konrat.

If you're stranded in the wild and need to employ natural first aid, "Mosses would be a great choice as an intermediary solution before you can get to a hospital," Martin says, adding,

"You can also put moss in your boots, and you won't have smelly feet."

"I'll give you one saying you can believe in," says Glime, spouting off the old maxim, "A rolling stone gathers no moss." That's really true. "At least in streams," Glime says, "Because once a rock is upside down the moss growing on it can't get any sunlight."

BOTTOM LINE: It can be fun to develop bushcraft skills such as natural navigation, but if you find yourself in a true survival situation, don't count on moss to guide you north. Keep in mind that the (mostly true) rule is that moss grows in damp places, and remember, too, that the best navigational tools are compasses and maps, plain and simple, so carry those whenever you're recreating outdoors.

Everything You Never Wanted to Know about Pooping Outdoors

Bears poop on the forest floor, so why can't we? Well, for starters, "Bears don't take Viagra, St. John's Wort, and penicillin," says Ben Lawhon, senior director of research and consulting for the Leave No Trace Center for Outdoor Ethics.

Pooping in the wilderness is one of Lawhon's favorite Leave No Trace topics. "It's something I'm well versed in," he says cheekily, and plus, as the childhood cult-classic *Everyone Poops* indicates, defecation is an unavoidable bodily function.

"The act of pooping is a means of getting rid of waste," explains Justin Chang, MD, an emergency medicine physician. While nearly all animals need to get rid of waste products, there are some interesting exceptions (sadly, that's beyond the scope of this chapter). "Humans, however, need to eliminate waste products either in the form of poop or pee," Chang continues.

Feces are mostly made up of water—"On average 75 percent," Chang says—plus bacteria. We also poop out various undigested food particles, and if we didn't eliminate these waste products, they'd build up in our bodies, eventually inter-fering with essential functions.

We all have our own unique bowel movement schedules. Some of us go two or three times a day, while others only feel the urge once every other day. Chang explains, "The frequency that people poop varies on a number of factors including diet, physiology, underlying medical conditions, environment, and personal habits."

Although there isn't a defined amount of time that a per-son could safely go without defecating, it's best to poop when the need arises. "Holding your poop for short periods of time can be okay, and sometimes necessary," Chang says. But people who make a habit of withholding stool for extended periods can develop all sorts of complications, ranging from chronic constipation to fecal impact or gastrointestinal tears.

According to the BBC, a sixteen-year-old woman in the United Kingdom died from a heart attack after eight weeks without a BM. That's an extreme example that drives home this next point: If the urge strikes, concede. "From a health and happiness standpoint," Chang says, "It is much better to have regular poops." For those who regularly defecate out-doors, good stewardship is key.

You're wrong if you believe that one person pooping on the surface just this one time isn't a big deal.

When it comes to wilderness poops, overabundance is the first topic to consider. According to the Outdoor Foundation's 2021 Outdoor Participation Report, 53 percent of Americans ages 6 and older participated in outdoor recreation at least once in 2020. That's the highest participation rate on record, with 7.1 million more Americans participating in outdoor recreation in 2020 than in the year prior.

With more and more people venturing outdoors, im-proper disposal of human waste has become a legit problem for land managers and outdoors enthusiasts alike. Imagine if even a fraction of outdoor participants pooped on the ground alongside the next trail you're planning to visit. Talk about an aesthetic nightmare.

It's pretty gross to accidentally stumble upon another hiker's pile of poo. Public health and hygiene, though, are much bigger concerns: If you and your kids aren't pooping responsibly, you could be contributing to the spread of diseases.

"Human feces have over a hundred different types of bacteria and viruses, and we shed millions of viral particles every time we go number two," Lawhon says. Our poop is full of bacteria and viruses, "both living and dead, either of which can cause disease," notes Chang.

"You could drink your own urine, that's actually totally fine, but if you eat poop you will get sick. Period. The end," says Dan Siegel, MD, a gastroenterology specialist. He talks ad nauseam about fecal-oral transmission, which is when the stool of a person infected with anything from e-coli to hepatitis or giardia ends up in another person's mouth. Consuming poop is "a really bad thing," as Siegel puts it.

But hey, it's not like you're planning to eat human feces if you stumble on an unsightly pile while recreating outside! Here's the problem with that line of thinking: "Feces left on the surface move," Lawhon explains.

Let's say you found a nice, secluded spot by a limber sapling that's way off the beaten path (see "What's the North Star Good for Anyway?" for notes on going off-trail) and you quickly dropped your high-tech, two-way-stretch hiking trousers and did your business on the ground, that is, "the surface," as Lawhon puts it. Yes, your poop will eventually vanish. "But it can take up to sixteen weeks for one pile to decompose to the point where harmful pathogens no longer exist," Lawhon explains.

And in the meantime, while those feces are breaking down on the ground, it's surprisingly easy for particles to spread beyond the initial dumpsite. The easiest way for bits of poop to travel is by water, mainly via rain and runoff. Siegel points out that "bacteria can easily be carried down into a nearby stream." Many outdoors enthusiasts already know the rule that you shouldn't poop or pee within 200 feet of a water source. But Mother Nature loves to complicate that general advice.

Water is constantly moving and changing. "Imagine somebody takes a dump on a rock in Utah, and then a quick thunderstorm rolls through," Lawhon says. Maybe there was a dry wash below the spot where he or she pooped. Or it looked like a dry wash. When the storm comes, the wash fills, and all those feces are flushed into an intermittent streambed. "From there, they can easily run into a creek, where they're carried to the Green River," says Lawhon.

It's also possible to spread feces through a forested environment. Fox, coyote, and other animals might put a paw in human poop, then track the stuff around, and Lawhon says, "Insects can land on human waste and fly off onto somebody's potato salad in a campground." You see the issue.

Take a deep breath and relax that sphincter: You can totally poop in the woods. It's just that unlike a bear, you can't poop on the forest floor. "Unskilled and uninformed behavior can have a negative impact," notes Lawhon. Luckily, it's pretty easy to poop responsibly, and Leave No Trace supplies outdoors enthusiasts with a series of simple techniques designed to protect the environment and everyone else who's outside enjoying it, too.

"I like to think of human waste disposal as a spectrum of options," Lawhon begins. On one end of that spectrum are flush toilets at, for example, a visitor center or possibly even a heavily trafficked trailhead. When recreating in the frontcountry, you might also find portable potties, vault toilets, and outhouses. If any of these amenities are available, use them before beginning your excursion.

"When we get into situations where these options don't exist, the next options are to pack out feces or dig a cat hole," says Lawhon. Outdoors enthusiasts should aim to "match the environment and their skill sets with local regulations," he adds.

In some specific areas, such as river corridors and very fragile ecosystems, it's illegal to leave human poop behind. Enter toilet kit waste bags, often called "wag bags." Available at REI and other outdoor retailers, these smell-proof containers allow users to capture poop in a big, puncture-resistant, zip-close bag with some special chemicals at the bottom to help solidify the waste. Individual kits come with a hand wipe and TP, and they're lauded for being user-friendly. "They're easy to carry, plus it's hard to mess them up," Lawhon says. In fact, he adds, "Wag bags have sort of become this gold standard for wilderness poops."

And yet it is a misconception that Leave No Trace wants people to pack out their own poop by collecting it in a plastic bag.

For some, the pack-out method is too disgusting to even attempt, and as long as you aren't recreating in an area where you're explicitly required to carry out your feces, it's totally acceptable to dig a cat hole.

A cat hole is a 6 to 8-inch-deep hole that recreationists can use in place of a toilet. The first step is to choose the right location. If you're camping, never poop in the same place twice, and if you're with a group, make sure everyone picks different areas. "When we put a lot of poop in the same place, it takes that much longer to break down," explains Lawhon. Dispersing feces into separate cat holes is an easy way to reduce your impact.

Cat holes should always be placed at least 200 feet from any water source, and keep in mind that even the tiniest creek counts as a water source. Steer clear of places where humans tend to recreate, including picnic areas, benches, trailheads, and campsites—because, yuck.

A good rule of thumb is to observe your surroundings, and then take 70 big steps away from any water sources and recreational spaces. Then do a 360-degree turn to see if there's a discrete spot with good, soft soil since digging a cat hole can be a real pain if the ground is hard, rocky, or full of roots. If there's a limber tree nearby, that'll be a huge bonus in a few minutes, when it's time to squat.

But first you've got to dig the hole. "A garden trowel is an ideal tool," Lawhon notes. Stash one in your backpack and remember that the trowel should always stay clean. "Your shovel never touches your poop," says Lawhon. If you're caught off-guard without a shovel, it's usually possible to break the ground with the heel of your shoe and then dig with a rock.

With whatever tools are available, dig a hole that's 6 to 8 inches deep and 4 to 6 inches in diameter (you know your needs best). But don't chuck all the soil over your shoulder while digging. This common mistake will make it tricky to cover up your hole later. Leave a pile of dug-up dirt right next to your hole.

Now you're ready. You can do this. "Relax, and try not to get stage fright," Lawhon says. Some shy recreationists might want to get a buddy to act as a lookout, and for novices, Lawhon recommends taking off underwear and pants entirely. "We hear of instances of accidental defecation in underwear, which is pretty messy in the outdoors," he notes.

A deep squat is an ideal position. "When your knees go above a certain angle, it helps straighten out your rectum," says Siegel, explaining that a special muscle that looks like a sideways V holds our poop in. The muscle relaxes when the knees are elevated, at which point, Siegel adds, "It's like an elbow straightening out."

When it comes to wiping, Lawhon says there are some major misconceptions surrounding toilet paper and Leave No Trace. Sure, in an ideal world everyone would pack out used TP, but for many of us that's as gross as packing out poop. It's totally fine if you're squeamish, Lawhon says, because there's an easy alternative: Bury TP deeply in your cat hole and forget about it.

If that's your plan, then be sure to carry a little commercial bathroom tissue in your backpack. The type of paper you choose (the fluffy at-home variety versus rapidly dissolving, biodegradable TP for RVs and boats) probably doesn't matter much. Recreational ecologist Jeff Marion, PhD, started a study on TP decomposition in a hilly, biodiverse Virginia forest in 2014. Marion and his co-researchers dug a bunch of cat holes and buried different types of toilet paper, as well as flushable and nonflushable disposable wipes.

Researchers have been digging up their specimens periodically to examine the soil. While the results of Marion's study haven't been published yet, Lawhon explains that "all traces of TP had vanished within a year, regardless of which brand of tissue was buried."

"If you have the option to get RV toilet paper, it will decompose faster, but if you like the thick stuff, that's fine, too, as long as you deal with it properly," Lawhon summarizes.

"A lot of people are curious about natural toilet paper," he continues. While Mother Nature's brand can be a viable option for adventurous folks, Lawhon recommends opting for tough, thick items such as unopened pinecones (pulled in the right direction!) and smooth stones over leaves. "Use a weak leaf one time, and you'll never do it again," he says. When conditions are prime, some pros will use snow ("Cold, but refreshing," Lawhon notes). No matter what option you land on, remember to always bury soiled items in the hole with the poop.

For all you A+ students, this next step is ideal but by no means mandatory. "For those brave enough to try it, we encourage people to make poop soup," Lawhon says. Basically, once you've buried your TP deeply inside the cat hole, use something other than your trowel—a stick, perhaps—to stir a little soil into the feces to initiate the breakdown process. But if the thought of poop soup makes you gag, don't bother. Simply move onto the last step of covering the hole.

Use the original dirt turned up while digging the cat hole, and make sure your trowel never touches your poop. "All the trowel does is dig," Lawhon reminds. If at any time you need to move your poop around, use a stick or a rock. Once your hole's covered, and the ground is level again, lightly stomp on the area, just to make sure everything is compacted. "In a forest, I'll put leaves or pine needles over the site," Lawhon says.

Hand washing is an important sanitation item to consider before you've even left your house, and I'm sorry to be the bearer of bad news, but there are some major misconceptions about hand sanitizer.

It's a myth that using hand sanitizer is a reliable substitute for old-fashioned hand washing with soap and water.

Stick with me, now, as we dive into some technical chemistry. Saponification is the process whereby soapers convert fat or oil into soap by using an alkali chemical. The result is a chemical structure—we call it soap—that resembles a balloon with a stringy tail. "One end of the structure, the balloon, has a type of electrical charge referred to as the 'polar' side," Chang says. Meanwhile, the other side (the tail) isn't charged. "It's called 'nonpolar,'" adds Chang, noting, "The importance of this is found in the phrase 'oil and water don't mix.'"

Remember the last time your bicycle chain slipped off its chainring, and your fingers got all greasy while addressing the problem? If you were out riding without access to soap, then you probably had a heck of a time getting the oil off your hands with water alone.

"When particles containing disease-causing bacteria or viruses get on our hands, they mix with the natural oil on our skin," Chang explains. And just like in our bike grease example above, the oily pathogens won't wash off easily with water alone. This is where the particles of soap come into play.

Soap has the characteristic of being both water-soluble and water-insoluble, so it can work to dissolve dirt and oil but also washes away with water. Since the soap's nonpolar end is grease and oil-soluble, Chang says, "It will stick to the grease or dirt on your hands, along with whatever bacteria or viruses they might have, while the polar end will be attracted to water molecules." And when enough soap surrounds the grease particles—voilà!—they'll easily wash away with water.

"The scrubbing that we do is helpful to agitate and displace the small bits of grease and dirt so that they get thoroughly surrounded by soap molecules," Chang continues. "And the water is needed to wash everything away," he says. So really, when it comes to hand washing, it's both soap and scrubbing that get rid of grease, dirt, and oil containing disease-causing bacteria and viruses. "There have been some studies to see whether hot or cold water is better when washing our hands, but it probably doesn't matter," Chang says. Having clean water is far more important than the water's temperature.

If you don't have access to soap and clean water, hand sanitizer might be better than nothing. "But it isn't necessarily adequate," Chang cautions, explaining that "hand sanitizers work differently than soap and water in that they don't actually help remove the grease and dirt containing bacteria and viruses." Instead, the alcohol in commercial hand sanitizers "acts by inactivating dangerous bacteria or viruses," Chang says. For this to happen, though, your hand sanitizer has to have *at least* 60 percent alcohol content, and you have to use a sufficient quantity to cover the entire surface of your hands.

"Even with that, there are some dangerous bacteria and viruses, such as cryptosporidium, norovirus, and clostridium difficile, all of which are common causes of diarrhea, that are not impacted at all by alcohol sanitizers," Chang adds. In these instances, only a thorough washing with soap and water will actually protect you. For best results, carry a small amount of biodegradable soap in your pack, wash your hands using spare water, and then follow up with hand sanitizer for extra oomph.

It's a myth that outdoors enthusiasts should mark their cat holes with sticks.

There's an urban legend about this floating around on the Internet, but Lawhon says, "It's a bogus notion." The whole idea is to disguise the area so there's absolutely no visual impact.

When it comes to pooping outdoors, a little prep goes a long way toward getting it right. Lawhon recommends putting together a small poop kit that includes a trowel, some TP, hand sanitizer, and a plastic bag. Stash the kit inside your daypack, and you won't have to worry about being caught off guard.

When recreationists aren't prepared to poop outside, they might end up making a split-second decision. If this happens, don't panic: It's possible to pull off a wilderness poop even when you're utterly unprepared.

It might take a little more finesse, but if you have to go number two, and you forgot to pack a trowel and TP, use a stick to dig and do your best with natural toilet paper. If there was an emergency, and you ended up having to poop on that ground, that's not such a big deal either. "Just dig your hole post-poo, push the feces into the hole, and cover the evidence," Lawhon advises.

For some people, it takes a while to get comfortable with the idea of pooping in the woods. As with anything new, go easy on yourself, and keep trying.

Now we know why human waste can't be left on the surface, and we also have a framework for dealing with our natural urges. But come on, there's plenty of scat on front- and backcountry trails. Is it really that important to pick up after a dog?

Quite simply: Yes. Pet waste has become a major pollutant across the United States. American dogs eliminate an estimated 10.6 million tons of poop every year. Dog feces taint water sources in urban, frontcountry, and backcountry areas, mainly because dog owners aren't always doing a stellar job picking up after their pups. Just like human poop, dog poop is filled with bacteria, and canine excrement has the potential to carry a variety of parasites: hookworms, roundworms, whipworms, giardia, salmonella, and parvo, to name a few.

Wild animals eat nutrients from their ecosystems—for instance, when elk eat wild berries—and return them into nature. As Lawhon puts it, "Dogs don't have a diet that's native to the environment." Their waste, then, is also nonnative. Most dogs eat processed food from a factory containing all sorts of additives. The addition of additive-filled poop to an ecosystem can cause a major imbalance, leading to toxic algae blooms in waterways and the growth of invasive plant species.

Lawhon also notes, "Research suggests that park visitors are often bothered when dog owners do not properly dispose of pet waste, and as a result conflict between visitors may arise."

The easiest solution is to pack out pet waste. If you forgot to pack a bag, or there aren't any trash cans in the area where you're recreating, dig a cat hole for your pet, Lawhon says, plain and simple.

In case you're curious, urine, generally speaking, doesn't have the same level of impact on the environment as feces. "But that doesn't mean it's not an issue," Lawhon says. One person walking off the trail, urinating at least 200 feet from a water source, isn't going to do any damage to the natural environment. "Urine usually becomes a hazard when it is concentrated," explains Lawhon, adding, "When everyone pees behind the same bush, that's when you start to have the unnatural accumulation of things like ammonia, urea, and uric acid."

Accumulated urine is usually more of an aesthetic issue given the odor. Large amounts of highly concentrated pee, though, can cause environmental impacts, especially to water sources. Scientists are just starting to observe pharmaceutical byproducts in backcountry water sources, and the working theory is that human urine is to blame. "There's some great research on this coming from Rocky Mountain National Park," Lawhon says, pointing to a 2012–2013 study on pharmaceuticals, hormones, pesticides, and other bioactive contaminants in the site's water and sediment.

"Researchers looked at backcountry water sources, both moving and still," Lawhon begins. In addition to collecting water and sediment, scientists also gathered some small animals, such as frogs and fish, from 20 sites inside Rocky Mountain National Park. Then they examined the specimens for various chemical compounds, including pharmaceuticals, hormones, and pesticides.

"They found traces of pharmaceutical drugs, including oxycodone," Lawhon reports. Water was also contaminated with caffeine and carbaryl, an insecticide. According to the researchers, these detected contaminants "are clearly attributable to direct local human input . . . [and] most of the 29 detected pharmaceuticals are excreted primarily in human urine, not feces." Bioactive contaminants definitely have the potential to harm local food webs by threatening native species. More research is needed on this specific topic.

A parting note on feminine hygiene: Pads and tampons don't occur naturally in the wild, so you'll have to pack them out. Burying these products isn't a good solution because, Lawhon says, "Tampons and pads just don't decompose in a reasonable time frame." For long-distance hikers using menstrual cups, the best practice is to pack out blood in a wag bag.

"But if you don't have a bag, and you can't pack out your blood, treat it like feces and go the cat hole route," Lawhon says, adding, "In terms of washing cups, we recommend taking water from a source, then walking at least 200 feet away to clean the menstrual cup."

BOTTOM LINE: Learn how to poop in the woods responsibly. YouTube videos are a great resource for novices, and sources such as Leave No Trace and REI also publish information on their websites. Once you've learned the basics, prepare a poop kit, stash it in your backpack, and you'll never look back. Always pick up after your pet, and don't pee near water sources.

The Supernatural Wonder
We Call Lightning

One of the spookiest things about lightning is that it can appear suddenly. In the blink of an eye, without much advance notice, a summer afternoon turns dark as warm air from the ground rises into the upper atmosphere. A storm picks up, and as it matures, anvil-shaped cumulonimbus clouds tower overhead, producing heavy rain and bright neon flashes.

It's a myth that lightning only strikes when it's raining or when clouds are visible overhead.

In August of 2014, the sky was clear and blue as Women's Wilderness field instructor Kris Norbraten and a co-instructor led a group of middle-school girls on a climbing expedition in Wyoming's Vedauwoo Climbing Area. Positioned on the iconic Nautilus formation, "There was no storm," Norbraten recalls, adding, "It wasn't even raining yet."

But since they'd seen a line of dark clouds in the distance, the instructors decided to call it a day, before any bad weather rolled in. In the early afternoon, the group packed up their equipment for the hike back to their van, stationed in the Nautilus parking lot. All eleven climbers were on and around a slab of rock when, seemingly out of nowhere, without a single clap of thunder as a heads up, a bolt of electricity traveled through the granite formation. "It went up whatever parts of our bodies were touching the rock," Norbraten recalls, adding, "Time disappeared for a moment. I had no idea what hit me."

While Norbraten's co-instructor suffered the worst physical injuries, almost everyone in the group was "knocked down by the voltage," Norbraten says. For several moments she couldn't see or hear anything. When the world came back into focus, she says, "It was as if we were inside the electricity." Norbraten was stunned. At first, nobody was sure what had just happened. Then, Norbraten says, everyone was screaming and crying.

The climbing instructors acted fast, rounding up their students. "Lined with mushroom-shaped boulders and open grassland," Norbraten says, "the trail leading back to the van was only a quarter-mile." But the walk felt much longer as the once-distant storm descended on the wounded climbers. Thankfully, everyone survived the ordeal.

"Lightning is one of the oldest observed natural phenomena on Earth," according to the National Weather Service. And it's also quite deadly. On average, floods are the only natural disaster to kill more people in the United States, where 30 to 40 lightning fatalities are recorded annually. Lightning injures far more Americans than it kills: The current data indicate that only about 10 percent of lightning victims will die. But since not all lightning victims report their injuries in a way that can be easily tracked, especially if they experience minor injuries, it is possible that these records aren't completely representative, notes Greg Schoor, severe weather program manager at the National Oceanic and Atmospheric Administration's National Weather Service.

While most victims survive lightning encounters, many are left with permanent and painful neurological damage, according to John Jensenius, a retired meteorologist nicknamed Dr. Lightning, formerly the National Weather Service's top lightning safety expert. Lightning wreaks havoc on the body's central nervous system, which is basically your own personal electrical wiring, similar to the cables running through a house. And yet a lightning encounter will impact different people in different ways. "Although a lightning victim might suffer intense burns, the greatest concern is the effect of lightning on the heart and neurosystem," Jensenius writes.

Many lightning victims also experience long-term ailments. As Norbraten puts it, "There's this really dark side to being struck by lightning." Immediately after her encounter, Norbraten felt "stunned, freaked out, scared, and hopped up on too much adrenaline," she says, adding, "My body was still buzzing." Lightning survival stories rarely account for lasting mental health impacts such as depression, suicide, and divorce.

The prolonged effects to Norbraten's systems were "akin to PTSD," she says. She became extremely reclusive after the accident. "I couldn't hike, climb, or even take my dog on a simple walk," Norbraten explains. Everything reminded Norbraten of lightning. "Phone flashes set me off, and so did the sound of garbage bins," she says. "Essentially, I went from climbing multipitch routes to being homebound, and I also became highly sensitive to stimulus, especially light and sound," she adds.

Pop culture, though, usually glosses over details like these, focusing instead on the incredible, seemingly supernatural events that have followed real-life lightning incidents. Take, for example, the fable about orthopedic physician Anthony Cicoria, who wrote his *Lightning Sonata* after a midlife zap in the 1990s inspired him to buy a piano.

Cicoria reported to multiple media outlets that he had no musical inclinations whatsoever before he was injured. And yet many reports failed to note that it took the doctor years of piano lessons and practice to become a composer. Cicoria's musical ingenuity wasn't an overnight miracle, as the story often goes.

For Norbraten, lightning opened the door to becoming a writer, but her new pathway wasn't totally out of the blue. Before her ordeal, Norbraten had studied English literature at Baylor University, so she definitely had a background in writing. Postaccident, she tried writing a short story "as a catharsis," she says, and the story morphed into a novel-length manuscript about a fading rock star in search of his lost voice and Sylvia, a woman with "a supernatural dose of lightning," Norbraten says.

Norbraten is always quick to point out that in real life, outside the library's fiction section, lightning is a powerful force of nature that can do serious damage and inflict major pain. One girl from Norbraten's group, for example, ended up with burns on her leg.

"It's almost like all of my nerves got totally cooked," Norbraten says. And that's a pretty good way to describe it since lightning is basically a gigantic electrical charge, Schoor points out. Ben Franklin proved this way back in 1752 with his infamous kite-flying experiment, wrote John Friedman in his book *Out of the Blue: A History of Lightning.*

"Lightning," Schoor elaborates, "is simply the discharge of electrostatic energy." In fact, the process that forms lightning is the same process that forms static electricity. You know that shock you sometimes feel when you touch a doorknob? If there is enough charge built up between your hand and the doorknob you're about to touch, then you don't even have to make direct contact in order for a discharge to occur. "You can get within an inch or so and feel a shock," Schoor explains. That's the same phenomenon as lightning, but on a *much* smaller scale.

The scientific term for the process that develops the cloud that will eventually produce lightning is "convection," which is a word some home chefs already know. Convection ovens speed up cooking by incorporating a fan and exhaust system that regular ovens lack. The fan inside a convection oven blows hot air over and around food, cooking it faster and more evenly. Whether we're talking about ovens or the atmosphere, "convection pushes air around in a way it's not used to, especially from lower levels of the atmosphere, up into the higher levels, and that generates turbulence," says Schoor.

Thunderstorms are prime examples of convective processes. As thunderclouds build in the sky, they grow taller and taller until eventually they tower, sometimes reaching heights of 8 miles, often poking up into the troposphere. Temperatures inside clouds can vary up to 100 degrees Fahrenheit, from bottom to top. That temperature difference helps to produce swift air currents, just like the ones in your handy home cooking device, transporting warmer air from down below to up high, making those cauliflower-looking clouds that seem to bulge out at the sides.

"For a lightning flash to occur, large areas of opposing electrical charges must exist within different parts of the cloud, as well as the Earth's surface," Schoor says. Scientists are still working to understand exactly *how* the requisite charge separation comes about. "Although the processes that generate charge separation are similar from thunderstorm to thunderstorm, the amounts, intensities, and relative spatial differences in regions of charge are not completely understood," adds Schoor.

Clouds are made up of very tiny water droplets called water vapor. During the convective process, you've got billions of water vapor droplets that can turn into ice crystals, and they're all surfing really intense air currents, bumping into each other, often generating friction that displaces electrons. One theory surrounding charge separation proposes that clouds become electrified as graupel and hail fall through water droplets and ice crystals.

"As the objects move through the cloud, the charge separation occurs," Schoor says, summarizing the hypothesis. Another supposition is that during the formation of precipitation, regions of separate charge exist within tiny cloud droplets and larger precipitation particles. "As the different forms of precipitation (solid, liquid, and gas) collide, charge separation occurs. The air currents that are generated within the cloud then transport the charges in ways that collect similar charges together," Schoor explains.

After a while, and for whatever reason, storm clouds are teeming with molecules with the wrong number of electrons. Some molecules have picked up extra electrons. These guys are called positive ions, and they gather at the top of the thundercloud. Meanwhile, molecules that lost electrons—that is, negative ions—meet up at the base of the cloud. This is nature's version of a giant floating battery.

"You've heard the term opposites attract?" Schoor asks. "That's definitely true in electromagnetism," he says. Positive and negative ions inside thunderclouds just want to connect with their better halves. "A vast majority of lightning flashes occur inside the cloud," Schoor says, and a very small percentage happens between thunderclouds and the ground below, as negative ions from the bottom of the cloud attempt to connect with positive ions on the Earth's surface.

This explains why it is a myth that lightning strikes the Earth from the sky.

Bolts of lightning aren't actually hitting the ground. In reality, the two different clusters of ions are simply trying to locate one another, often connecting midair via the path of least resistance. As the charge from the tippy-top of a radio tower, let's say, goes up, the charge from a cloud is simultaneously traveling down. When the two groups of ions meet, we see a large neon bolt. And that bolt appears to be "striking" the ground.

Your eyes are tricking you. "If we could slow down a flash, we'd see that lightning actually moves from the sky and the ground," says Schoor. Often, the charge that reaches upward from the surface is not as strong as the portion that's coming downward from the cloud. "So it's not as if they meet halfway, necessarily. Instead, that charge dispersion is realized not too far up above the ground," Schoor adds.

The scientific community has moved away from the term "lightning strike." If you want to be scientific, use the term "lightning flash," and note that lightning victims are zapped, buzzed, grazed, and harmed by lightning, not stricken.

There are a few different ways a person can be zapped, but the most common is through a ground current, which occurs when a lightning flash flows through an object such as a tree, releasing its energy onto the ground.

Anyone standing in the vicinity of a flash could potentially be impacted by a ground current, and ground currents can even travel onto porches and garage floors, which is why experts warn, "When thunder roars, go indoors." If you hear thunder, that's your warning that there's lightning nearby and it's time to find shelter.

Norbraten was lucky to survive her ordeal. Between 2006 and 2019, 418 people in the United States died by lightning, with around 62 percent of those engaging in "leisure activities," including rock climbing. Not surprisingly, water-based activities—fishing, boating, swimming, and recreating at the beach—engendered the most deaths, according to data issued by the National Lightning Safety Council and National Weather Service. Forty people died fishing, while camping deaths amounted to just half that, totaling 20 fatalities over the course of the study.

While water doesn't attract electricity, it's a conductor, just like metal, so wet areas provide a convenient path for lightning to follow. According to geoscientist Elizabeth Gordon, professor and chair of Earth and Geographic Sciences at Fitchburg State University, "Lightning is one of the most underrated weather hazards," and it's also one of the least understood acts of nature.

If you associate lightning solely with thunderstorms, you're not totally off base.

"When there is thunder there is always lightning, even if you can't see it," wrote Lisa Densmore in her pocket guide *Predicting Weather: Forecasting, Planning and Preparing.*

Though lightning is commonly seen in thunderstorms, it occurs in other scenarios, too. "You don't need moisture, or a specific temperature, or anything like that for lightning to form," Schoor says. All that's required is the turbulent process of convection, and lightning has been present in volcanic eruptions, extraordinarily hot forest fires, large hurricanes, and even blizzards—yes, blizzards—although the latter is a pretty rare occurrence that usually happens in nor'easters coming in from the North Atlantic Ocean.

Despite modern technology, there's still a lot we don't know about lightning, and some lightning myths are hard to debunk because, as Norbraten points out, "Scientists and meteorologists are still confounded by lightning."

Scientists, for example, love to debate the temperature of lightning, and some websites claim lightning can reach 50,000 degrees Fahrenheit, which is five times hotter than the surface of the sun. "In studies scientists have done, temperature has been all over the map," Schoor points out.

The problem is that lightning is crazy-difficult to study. Meteorologists can't see the forces that create lightning, and on top of that, it's almost impossible to predict when and where it will occur. When there is a flash, it's over in, well, a flash. All these factors make field research really challenging.

At the end of the day, Schoor concludes that "lightning is mysterious." For now, it remains an extreme weather phenomenon bridging the gap between our natural and supernatural worlds. And yet for all the mystery, there are some life-saving truths the experts know for certain.

It's safe to touch somebody who has just been injured by lightning.

"Some people are under the mistaken impression that when somebody's zapped, they're filled with an electric charge," Schoor says. That's completely false. "You can't die or become injured by touching a lightning victim," Schoor reiterates. The science is simple: Human bodies are not a container for electric charge. When lightning enters a body, it exits within a microsecond.

So if lightning injures a friend, help immediately by checking for a pulse, calling 911, and talking to the victim until help arrives. If the person isn't breathing, perform CPR, but don't move them, Schoor warns, since this can cause further damage.

The best thing to do is avoid a lightning encounter altogether. Outdoors enthusiasts should always check the local weather forecast before recreating outside. If storms are predicted, be flexible. Reschedule your activity, hit the trail earlier, or at the very least, decide what you'll do if a storm appears while you're still outside.

If you see a thunderstorm approaching, it's possible to estimate the lightning's distance by counting seconds. Humans have tried forecasting weather since the dawn of time, and some old wives' tales are strangely accurate. For example, it really is true that you can determine how far away a thunderstorm is by counting the seconds between a lightning flash and its accompanying thunder.

We see lightning before hearing thunder because light travels faster than sound. When you see a flash, count by thousandths—that is, one one-thousandth, two one-thousandths ... Each one-thousandth will be about a second, and for every five seconds, the storm is a mile away.

"The magic number is five," Schoor says. Divide the number of seconds you counted by five to determine the distance, in miles, to the lightning bolts. If you see lightning and then hear thunder 10 seconds later, the lightning is about 2 miles away (10 ÷ 5 = 2).

The method is an approximation, Schoor notes, but it works well for those in need of a simple rule of thumb. For more precise information, carry a NOAA weather radio or a portable AM radio, available at most electronics stores, and you'll have up-to-date weather forecasting at your fingertips.

A thunderstorm is always a threat, but if you're caught in one, don't panic. Try to get indoors ASAP. The safest places to hunker down are enclosed structures with electrical wiring and plumbing, which conduct electricity much more efficiently than the human nervous system. If you're inside a house, school, office building, or shopping center, lightning will discharge through the building's systems rather than through you.

"Don't seek shelter in a metal shed," Schoor warns. Exposed and open structures are also unsafe: Avoid beach shacks, picnic pavilions, baseball dugouts, carports, and porches.

Cars and trucks, on the other hand, are smart options. It might seem counterintuitive since they're made of metal, but if you're inside an automobile with the windows up, the vehicle acts as a Faraday cage, Schoor explains, referring to enclosures that can be used to block electromagnetic fields. When lightning zaps a car, the charge goes around the sides and out the bottom, and anyone inside should be safe, so long as they aren't touching metal.

Tents offer absolutely no protection from lightning. None. Campers should avoid pitching their tents on hills and ridgetops, as well as in open fields. If possible, set up camp in a low area, such as a valley or ravine, and never seek shelter from a thunderstorm under a tree. Tall timber is nature's version of a lightning rod, and when lightning zaps a tree, the electrical current can radiate to nearby objects and people.

It's a myth that crouching provides protection from lightning.

For those caught outdoors, the standard advice used to be to crouch on the ground. Schoor remembers, "Old timey graphics showing a person crouched with their rear end hanging in the air." But this so-called lightning crouch is decades outdated.

When positive and negative ions connect on the Earth's surface, lightning branches out along the ground, sometimes for hundreds of feet. Crouching won't significantly lower your odds of being injured, but if there's absolutely no other option, Schoor recommends getting as low as possible by retreating into a ditch or ravine. Move away from anything that's a conductor of electricity, too, mainly water, metal, and electronic devices connected to a wire. Your iPhone13 shouldn't pose too much risk: Just don't hold it up in the air really high like you're trying to flag somebody down.

Exposed ridges and mountaintops are two terrible places to get caught in a thunderstorm. If you're above tree line, and you can't rush below, move away from the highest point immediately. "Get away from your pack, it probably has metal in it," Schoor advises, and avoid wet areas. Also, have everyone in your group fan out 25-plus feet from each other to reduce the chance of everyone being zapped.

Since the vast majority of lightning injuries and fatalities happen on boats, those who plan to recreate on water really need to check the forecast before their adventure. If meteorologists predict thunderstorms, the solution is simple: Don't go out. "Just have a backup plan," says Schoor. If you're on open water and see a storm forming, head back to the shore—immediately. When land is too far, "stow your paddle or oars parallel to the water (not sticking up) and get as low as possible in the middle of the boat, avoiding contact with wet objects," writes Lisa Densmore.

It's definitely a myth that lightning never strikes the same place twice.

You've probably heard the old adage that "lightning never strikes the same place twice." While he's not sure where the saying originated, Schoor has heard that it was coined in the 1850s, way before the advent of technology such as slow motion cameras, which have given modern meteorologists the ability to actually see lightning zapping the same place twice.

"I've heard the old saying was simply meant as maxim," Schoor says, "Meaning you could never have something so good or so bad happen twice." While the sentiment might hold true, the saying has no scientific basis. Schoor points to the Empire State Building. When a thunderstorm rolls through Midtown Manhattan, the massive copper lightning rod at the tip of New York City's iconic, towering structure can be zapped dozens of times in just one storm.

The saying *lightning never strikes twice* implies that lightning is a rare occurrence. The truth is, lightning is very common. "At any given moment, there can be as many as 2,000 thunderstorms occurring across the globe," says Schoor. This translates to over 14.5 million storms annually, and NASA satellite research indicates that these storms produce lightning flashes about 40 times per second. "This is a change from the commonly accepted value of 100 flashes per second, which is an outdated estimate from 1925," notes Schoor.

Lightning is one of the leading causes of weather-related fatalities, according to the Centers for Disease Control, but your odds of being injured in a given year are only about 1 in 500,000. Over a lifetime (estimated at 80 years), Americans have a 1 in 15,300 chance of being zapped, according to the National Weather Service. By contrast, the chances you'll win the lottery during your lifetime are roughly 1 in 175 million. This data was based on information gathered between 2009 and 2018 and uses a 2019 US population estimate of 330 million. "You're significantly more likely to be struck by lightning than win the lottery. Don't buy a ticket," according to the National Weather Service.

"The thing to keep in mind is that an average is a watered down number," Schoor says. If you're reading this book, you're probably an outdoorsy person, and your odds of encountering lightning might be significantly higher than those of your friend who hates spending time in nature. Also, if your favorite pastimes include boating or golf, you're much more likely to be injured by lightning than, say, a bowler.

Where you live also plays a significant role in your odds of experiencing a lightning injury, and there are even seasonal considerations. Florida, for instance, is the lightning capital of the country, recording 468 deaths between 1959 and 2012, according to National Weather Service data. (Texas ranks second with 215.)

More specifically, the central Florida peninsula, from Tampa Bay to Cape Canaveral, has the highest lightning concentration in the country, and more than 90 percent of the lightning here occurs between May and October, between noon and midnight. People who routinely recreate outdoors in Florida during these periods are significantly more likely to be zapped than, say, a person who spends the majority of their day in a region like the Pacific Northwest, where thunderstorms are few and far between.

BOTTOM LINE: The threat of lightning shouldn't keep you from enjoying the great outdoors, and yet it's good to have a healthy respect for one of Mother Nature's most powerful forces.
If a storm approaches, take shelter and wait it out. Most of the time, a passing thunderstorm is just that. Let it pass and then you can move on with your activities. When the thunder roars, go indoors: This is the best lightning-related adage to remember, and it will help keep you safe from an extreme weather phenomenon that scientists are only now beginning to understand.

How to Keep Warm in the Bitter Cold

The man sat down on his blankets in a crouching position
. . . his head on his knees advertised that he had given up
the struggle. Now and again he raised his head to note the
dying down of the fire. The circle of flame and coals was
breaking into segments with openings in between. These
openings grew in size, the segments diminished. "I guess
you can come an' get me any time," he mumbled. "Anyway,
I'm goin' to sleep."
   —A description from Jack London's *White Fang*, regarding
      a man alone in the freezing cold, surrounded by wolves
      (see "Wolves, Explained"), with his fire about to go out

A few years ago, wilderness EMT Erik Kulick was leading a
group of six students through the rugged Quebec Run Wild
Area, on the western edge of the Appalachians, as part of a
two-night course offered through the True North Wilderness
Survival School. "It was April, so technically it was spring-
time," Kulick recalls. But it had been raining and snowing all

day, and conditions north of the Maryland border were "just miserable," as Kulick puts it.

Kulick's introductory field classes are designed to teach outdoors enthusiasts basic principles of wilderness survival, and this particular cohort was about to learn a valuable lesson about preventing disasters before they ever arise. As the group trudged through unpleasant conditions, Kulick noticed that enthusiasm levels had sagged in a major way. "People stopped talking, and they were slower in their steps," he remembers. Sensing that the cold, wet weather was taking a toll on his students, Kulick decided to reverse course: Rather than continue hiking, as planned, he made camp.

"I decided to make a fire, too," he recalls (see "Do Campfires Serve a Purpose?"). "It was a teeny, small flame initially, but everyone got in close, and pretty soon people were laughing, making jokes, and there was a substantial psychological change," says Kulick. He talks about an early warning sign of cold-weather danger, "the umbles," explaining, "First you grumble, then you mumble."

"Cold is a far greater threat to survival than it appears," as stated in chapter 15 of the US Department of the Army's 1957 field manual, *Survival, FM 21-76*, one of 500-plus US Army field manuals currently in circulation. Detailed army guides contain information on a range of topics related to survival in very harsh environments, and while they're printed specifically for soldiers serving in the field, they've become popular among civilians, too, mainly avid backpackers, extreme athletes, and outdoors enthusiasts looking to brush up on wilderness survival skills.

Survival, FM 21-76 has been updated periodically since its initial 1950s run, with guides such as *Survival, FM 21-76* (June 1992) and *FM 3-05.70* (May 2002). But not much has changed in chapter 15, titled "Basic Principles of Cold Weather Survival."

According to *Survival, FM 21-76*, cold weather "decreases your ability to think and weakens your will to do anything except to get warm." The cold is described by the US Army as "an insidious enemy; as it numbs the mind and body, it subdues the will to survive."

That last bit is really important. "Having the will to survive is just as critical as having any basic need covered," Kulick says. *Survival, FM 21-76* corroborates Kulick's viewpoint, stating, "There have been incidents when trained and well-equipped individuals have not survived cold weather situations because they lacked the will to live."

The manual goes on to provide a series of important and accurate tips for maximizing warmth. But the text also includes a statement that has been cited so frequently that it has perhaps evolved into one of the most well-known outdoor myths in existence.

The manual reads, "Always keep your head covered. You can lose 40 to 45 percent of body heat from an unprotected head and even more from the unprotected neck, wrist, and ankles." A restatement of the figure (40 to 45 percent) also appears in another military guide, *Survival, Evasion, and Recovery* (June 1999), drawing information from several sources, including *Survival, FM 21-76*, as well as Marine Corps and Navy Warfare publications on survival.

It's a myth that humans lose nearly half of their body heat through the head.

Since a typical human head accounts for about 7 percent of the body's total surface area, this would mean that our heads lose roughly 20 times as much heat per square inch than other body parts. If that sounds like bunk, well, it is.

At most, a person loses 7 to 10 percent of their body heat through their head, according to a 2008 report in the *British Medical Journal* written by two professors of pediatrics, Rachel Vreeman and Aaron Carroll.

The figure cited in *Survival, FM 21-76*, though, wasn't just some random number. Back in the 1950s, the US military did a study on heat loss, and according to Vreeman and Carroll, the head-heat-loss myth is "thought to have arisen through a flawed interpretation of a vaguely scientific experiment by the U.S. military."

For the experiment, army researchers dressed volunteers in Arctic survival suits then exposed them to freezing-cold temperatures. While the subjects' bodies were adequately bundled, their heads were fully exposed, leading onlookers to "discover" that most of the body's heat escapes through the noggin.

Are you having a big ah-ha moment? "Because it was the only part of their bodies left uncovered, most of their heat was lost through their heads," Vreeman and Carroll wrote. "If the experiment had been performed with people wearing only swimming trunks, they would have lost no more than 10 percent of their body heat through their heads," the scientists concluded.

If you've been enduring itchy wool hats since childhood because your parents and grandparents worried about all your body's heat escaping through your head, you can send your complaints to the US Army. The science is simple: "You will lose heat from whatever body parts are exposed," says Lindy Rossow, PhD, assistant professor of Exercise Science at Maryville University of St. Louis. Oftentimes, that's your head. As Rossow points out, "I'm not going outside in the snow without pants, but I might go outside without a hat."

Even though the 40 to 45 percent figure is flawed, the US Army's advice to wear a hat shouldn't be dismissed. The more body parts you can cover, the less heat you'll lose, and as Kulick points out, "If you're wearing inappropriate clothing for the weather, at a minimum you might feel really uncomfortable." (At worst, choosing the wrong gear could beget the onset of hypothermia.)

Covering your head while recreating outside in cold weather can greatly increase subjective comfort, and since cold weather survival is intricately linked to a person's mental state, feeling comfortable is really important. What's more, even though we might not lose 45 percent of our body's heat through our heads, the face and head are definitely more sensitive to changes in temperature than the rest of the body. Noses, ears, cheeks, and chins, along with extremities such as fingers and toes, are most vulnerable to frostbite.

A human head has way less protective tissue (i.e., fat and muscle) compared to, say, a torso, and so will struggle to maintain the body's core temperature in cold environments. But that's not the only factor at work.

Similar to a home furnace, our bodies regulate temperature by maintaining a tight balance between heat gain and loss. Your core temperature should fall somewhere between 97.7 and 99.5 degrees Fahrenheit. A region of the forebrain called the hypothalamus regulates this, along with a few other things, by listening to temperature receptors located throughout the body and then making physiological adjustments to account for external elements such as cold air and wind. If you're mountain biking on a hot day, temperature receptors in the skin send signals to the hypothalamus, and it sends out the message that it's time to sweat.

By contrast, when the air is cold, your peripheral blood flow diminishes as your body constricts the vasculature in the extremities to minimize heat loss. When your body gets so cold that its core temperature begins to drop below the ideal range, the hypothalamus is forced to make a game-time decision: Rather than route blood into the limbs, your brain can instruct the heart to pump blood to important vital organs like the lungs and heart. In the grand scheme of things, Kulick notes, "Your fingers, toes, and the tip of your nose aren't that important," and so these areas are much more likely to become frostbitten.

Keeping the core warm is critical in a cold weather survival situation because that's where all your vital organs are located.

There are four processes by which a human body can lose heat, but when it comes to cold weather, our body's heat is typically lost through convection. "Our bodies generate a layer of heat around them," Rossow explains. "As they move through air or water, that layer is disturbed, and this disturbance of the 'air bubble' surrounding us is termed 'convection,'" she adds.

With modern gear, we can prevent convection from stripping us of our warmth. "Clothing traps air by your body and stops air from moving away," Rossow explains. "Down is the perfect example of something that ically keeps heat trapped next to the body, creating an insulative layer to prevent heat loss."

Not all natural fibers adequately protect us from the cold. Cotton, for example, is a no-no. Most outdoors enthusiasts have heard the saying, "Cotton kills." The science behind the slogan is simple: Cotton is a cellulosic fiber obtained from plants. "As such, it's built to absorb and retain moisture," explains Jordan Todoroff, the head of sales for Ibex, a Vermont-based manufacturer of ethical outdoor performance apparel.

Picture a vascular plant's stem. This structural powerhouse contains special cells—the xylem—that form long, thin tubes used in transporting water from the soil throughout a plant's stalk. Thanks to xylem, cotton can retain up to 27 times its own weight in moisture. "That means a one-pound cotton garment, fully saturated, could weigh up to 28 pounds," says Todoroff.

In warm and hot climates, this can cause discomfort—chafing, for example, or a garment that feels heavy. But there's no real danger. And, in fact, the evaporative cooling might even seem like a benefit for some athletes. Cold conditions, though, are a different story.

"As you start to work up a sweat, cotton absorbs that moisture," Todoroff begins. And if you encounter precipitation, such as rain or snow, cotton will suck that up, too. If the temperature drops during your adventure, the water held within the fibers will begin to freeze next to your skin. "Without a change of clothes, or a readily available heat source, hypothermia can set in within a matter of minutes," Todoroff notes.

Despite cotton's flaws, it's a common misconception that synthetic gear outperforms natural fibers in cold-weather environments.

When it comes to creating outdoor performance apparel that will function well in cold weather, manufacturers are primarily concerned with moisture management. "A textile needs to have two primary characteristics. It needs to be moisture wicking and quick drying," says Todoroff.

Moisture-wicking fabrics pull sweat away from the skin, whereas quick-drying fabrics will release excess moisture. "While these two properties are often grouped together, the characteristics can be mutually exclusive," Todoroff notes.

The most common quick-drying and moisture-wicking fabrics available are polyester, nylon, acrylic, polypropylene, silk, and wool. Synthetic fibers (polyester, nylon, acrylic, and polypropylene) exploded in popularity from the 1960s into the 1980s, and they still dominate the outdoor apparel industry. In the United States, roughly 60 percent of the clothing we wear is now synthetic.

Synthetics have some pros: They're cheap to produce and are usually very durable, plus they have performance qualities we love since they wick moisture, dry quickly, and stretch with our bodies. "However, at their heart, they're still petroleum-based synthetics, derived from fossil fuels," Todoroff points out. They're not biodegradable, and their smooth fibers encourage bacterial growth. Even after a small amount of sweat, synthetic gear can really stink.

With synthetic fabrics, Todoroff explains, "The fiber itself is not providing warmth." By keeping the body dry, manufactured fibers allow your skin to temperature-regulate, and that's what ultimately keeps you comfortable in chilly weather.

Natural fibers such as wool and silk are different. And merino wool, in particular, easily outperforms synthetic fabrics in several categories. As Todoroff puts it, "Merino sheep are thought to possibly be the oldest breed of sheep in the world, so nature has spent an immense amount of time and effort perfecting this fiber."

At about one-fifth the diameter of a human hair, merino fibers are incredibly fine with natural elasticity. Merino sheep live in climates that range from 95 degrees Fahrenheit in the summer down to −4 degrees Fahrenheit in the winter. "Nature has designed the fiber to keep the wearer cool in the heat and warm in the cold," adds Todoroff.

The effect of wearing wool in cold weather is similar to that of a wetsuit. "Wool can actually release a small amount of heat when changing from a dry environment to a wet or humid one, and wool also uses a small amount of moisture within the core of the fiber to keep the body warm," says Todoroff.

Smartwool chooses to work with Merino wool because it's "pretty darn perfect for every adventure regardless of season," adds Maggie Meisinger, a spokesperson for the company. "When it's cold outside, the natural crimps and bends in wool's fibers trap air, insulating you," she notes. Synthetic fibers cannot crimp and bend like this.

Merino is not only biodegradable, but fully compostable. "And finally, the thing everyone loves most about merino is that it naturally prevents bacterial growth caused by human sweat," Todoroff says. Tiny keratin plates cover the surface of each fiber, making it nearly impossible for bacteria to grow and spread. On top of that, the chemical compounds found within the core of the fiber neutralize odor.

Even a mild case of hypothermia can be dangerous when recreating outdoors.

Whether you prefer wool or synthetic fibers, having the right gear is especially important when recreating outdoors in chilly, wet weather, because adding moisture to cold air greatly increases one's risk of developing the life-threatening condition hypothermia.

In Kulick's experience, "even people who are only mildly to moderately hypothermic tend to make bad decisions." Emergencies aren't usually about one thing that went wrong, but rather a chain of things. Hypothermia accelerates bad decisions. For example, if you're out hiking and the air turns cool, then wet, you might want to get back to the trailhead as quickly as possible, so you can crank up the heat in your car. "People are often tempted to take a shortcut, and when the path they choose isn't the shortcut they thought it was, now your situation is becoming critical," Kulick says.

As stated in a 2002 version of the army's field manual on survival, "Hypothermia is the lowering of the body temperature at a rate faster than the body can produce heat." The prefix, *hypo*, translates "low," and *thermia* is Greek for "heat," explains Rossow. "The word hypothermia is literally defined as a drop in core body temperature," she says.

When it comes to temperature, our bodies strive for consistency. The gold standard is 98.6 degrees, though as noted above, temperatures between 97.7 and 99.5 will work just fine. "When we start to deviate from our body's desired temperature, we become hypothermic," Kulick explains.

If you're exposed to cold air for a prolonged period of time, or you suddenly become wet on a cool or cold day, your core temperature can begin to change. Rossow notes, "Cold water is much more dangerous than cold air." But either way, if you don't "stop this deviation," as Kulick puts it, by becoming warm again, then your physical state can deteriorate quickly.

"The initial symptom is shivering," according to *Survival, FM 21-76*. Shivering begins when the body's core temperature falls and is the body's way of generating heat through rapid muscle contraction, Rossow explains. At about 95 degrees, you'll devolve into what's called mild hypothermia, and even this condition can be surprisingly dangerous.

As your core temperature dips toward 90 degrees Fahrenheit, "sluggish thinking, irrational reasoning, and a false feeling of warmth may occur." Hypothermia causes everything to slow down. "Blood flow to the brain is minimized as your body focuses on keeping vital organs going," says Rossow, adding, "This could explain why people start making bad decisions when hypothermic." Some scientists have posited that the brain temperature itself lowers, prohibiting optimal performance. "These are just speculations," Rossow says.

The treatment for hypothermia is to rewarm the entire body. The more time that passes without getting warm, the more dire the situation becomes. But here's the really baffling thing about hypothermia: There's no specific core temperature at which a human body will perish from the cold. Using cold water immersion baths, Nazi doctors hypothesized that death occurs when a human's core temperature drops to 77 degrees, and the US Army has corroborated this figure in its survival manuals, stating, "If the victim's core temperature falls below . . . 77 degrees F, death is almost certain."

And yet the lowest recorded core temperature in a surviving adult was 56.7 degrees, observed in then-29-year-old radiologist Anna Bågenholm after she fell into a frozen stream during a ski trip in Norway in May of 1999. Death by hypothermia is "really individualized," as Rossow puts it. It's possible that a high level of muscle mass is beneficial in cold weather survival, but really, there's just no surefire way to predict how quickly, and in whom, hypothermia will strike.

"In hypothermia, we have constriction of the vasculature in fat tissue," Rossow begins. Scientists have a way of making concepts sound overly complicated, but if we avoid getting bogged down in jargon, it's really pretty simple. In laymen's terms, Rossow says, "Humans can't really mobilize fat very well, so when we're hypothermic we end up relying more on glucose as a fuel source."

The problem is, the average person's glucose reserves are significantly smaller than their fat reserves. When a person succumbs to hypothermia, it's not that they ran out of fuel. "They just got so cold that their body couldn't function anymore," Rossow says.

Throughout history, native populations have sometimes developed fascinating adaptations to the cold. Inuit people and Norwegian fishers, for example, frequently work gloveless in freezing temperatures. They don't experience frostbite or hypothermia, though, because of the hunting response, a phenomenon whereby chilled hands can open their surface capillaries intermittently, thus supplying warm blood to cold extremities, elevating skin temperature within minutes.

For most of us, though, the body's only recourses are to shiver or become active. Shivering and movement will cause the body to produce heat, but eventually, these activities also cause fatigue. A passage from *Survival, FM 21-76* reads, "It has been noted that a naked man exposed to still air at or about 0 degrees C (32 degrees F) can maintain a heat balance if he shivers as hard as he can." The guide goes on to point out the obvious: We can't shiver forever. "When the shivering mechanism shuts down, things are not looking good in terms of survival," Rossow says.

While training students in the art of survival, Kulick has seen firsthand that there are "a whole lot of misconceptions about hypothermia," he says. For the sake of safety, he lists a number of potentially dangerous myths.

It's a myth that hypothermia is a winter problem.

Writers for the USDA Forest Service explain, "Hypothermia is most likely at very cold temperatures, but it can occur even at cool temperatures above 40 degrees Fahrenheit if a person becomes chilled from rain, sweat, or submersion in cold water." In fact, milder temperatures can sometimes be more dangerous to recreationists than freezing-cold weather because in, say, the middle of July, most people aren't expecting hypothermia to strike.

"But what if it suddenly rains and you become chilled?" Kulick asks. Hypothermia is just as capable of striking on a cool spring afternoon as on a snowy winter day. And speaking of snow . . .

It's a myth that you can treat hypothermia or frostbite by rubbing snow on your skin.

If you're out in the cold, and sense you're becoming hypothermic, don't rub snow on your body, no matter what you've heard. "This is actually a more commonly held belief than you'd think," Kulick begins. If your toes are cold and become pained, and then you're unable to feel them, you might be tempted to take a handful of snow and rub it on those digits. "It doesn't work," says Kulick.

For one, you'd be making your extremities colder by rubbing something cold on them, but more important, Kulick says, "You don't ever want to rub moderately to severely frostbitten digits because you'll risk rupturing the tissue."

Sorry to be the bearer of sad news, but it's a myth that whiskey will warm you up.

"Whiskey makes you *feel* warm," Kulick says—so does hot cocoa!—"but it doesn't do anything functionally." In fact, drinking whiskey or warm liquid when you're still stranded outside in the cold could actually have a negative impact on your health. If your brain gets tricked into thinking the body is being warmed, it will start sending blood back to your limbs, diverting lifesaving warmth from your core. You'd be better off trading that finger of whiskey for a Snickers bar since simple sugar and fat can provide some temporary fuel for your body's furnace, Kulick says.

To effectively treat hypothermia, though, you'll have to rewarm the entire body, which can be tough to do outside of a medical facility. So really, the best cure for hypothermia is prevention, and the best prevention is to stop exposure. "First, change the environment from cold and wet to warm and dry," says Kulick. "Move indoors or erect a shelter, and change wet clothes to dry, if possible."

If somebody in your group is a victim of mild to moderate hypothermia, Kulick warns, "Don't give them anything hot to drink." Once you've made them a shelter, "Fuel the furnace by hydrating and eating," Kulick says. Push hydration drinks (Kulick always carries powdered mixes) and discourage them from rigorous movement.

"Many people are told to jog in place, or physically exert themselves, but that's not the best thing," says Kulick, noting that while movement can produce warmth, it also causes the body to sweat, and if this happens, you could wind up losing even more heat through evaporation.

"Put the person in a sleeping bag, and try to get them warm with warm water bottles on either side of the neck, in the armpits, and around the genitals," Kulick advises, adding, "As the person starts feeling better, have them do light activity that won't produce sweat." Sit-ups can be a good option. But don't shed all your warm clothing and hop into the bag with your buddy. While skin-to-skin contact might have psycho-logical benefits, Kulick says, "It's usually not worthwhile since, through the process of conduction, the patient will make the rescuer's body colder."

Last but not least, it's a myth that you don't have to drink as much water when it's cold out.

Sustaining adequate hydration is essential for normal bodily functions, and yet many outdoors enthusiasts fail to associate dehydration with hypothermia. Especially when it's very dry and cold, humans lose a lot more water than you'd think. If you're cross-country skiing, snowshoeing, or engaging in another wintertime sport, you're probably sweating, losing body heat through evaporation, even if you can't feel it.

In addition to wearing layers that can be taken off to prevent excess sweating, drink more water than you think you need to replace any fluid lost through sweat. As the US Army points out, "Your need for water is as great in a cold environment as it is in a warm environment."

BOTTOM LINE: One of the most difficult situations any outdoor enthusiast can face is cold weather survival. You'll lose heat through whatever areas of your body aren't properly covered, and while the right gear can help ward off hypothermia, nothing beats knowledge, common sense, and preparation.

The Secret Lives of Sharks

"I'd grown up fishing in South Carolina, but I'd never seen a shark up close," says shark biologist Jasmin Graham, MS, president and CEO of Minorities in Shark Sciences. Graham vividly recalls her first shark encounter as an undergraduate at the College of Charleston. Graham and a few peers were collecting samples as part of a long-term gillnet survey project assessing the species makeup of Charleston Harbor and its tributaries.

"Same as a lot of people, I'd had this image of sharks being big," Graham says. But the first shark she held was a baby bonnethead shark, no bigger than a soprano-sized ukulele. "My initial thought was, 'Wow! That's an itty-bitty thing,'" Graham recalls. A moment later, though, the scientist's mind was filled with more technical observations.

The feel of the shark's rough skin caught Graham off-guard. "I'd touched dolphins and stingrays before, and this was different," she says. Graham held the shark while measuring it and placing an identification tag on it. During that time, another thought struck Graham: "The shark hadn't tried to bite me," she says.

Since her first shark experience in 2014, Graham says, "I've worked with lots of sharks, hundreds in fact, and I have yet to be bitten." Graham swims with sharks, too, and relishes solo snorkels, when she can get really still and watch a leopard shark, for example, off the coast of California—"They are the epitome of poise and grace," she says—or float in the shadow of the biggest fish in the sea, the whale shark, which is always a spiritual experience for Graham.

"Watching sharks swim is incredibly peaceful," Graham continues. With just a tiny little flick of the tail, there they go, gliding easily through the water. Having an opportunity to swim among sharks is "euphoric," according to Marie Levine, executive director of the Shark Research Institute, a decades-old organization aimed at safeguarding sharks while correcting misperceptions.

But the experiences described above don't exactly correspond with prevailing public opinion. Sharks are one of the most feared creatures in the entire animal kingdom, and the media routinely portrays them as vicious, bloodthirsty monsters. Yet, Levine points out, "Driving to the beach is more dangerous than swimming among sharks."

It's a myth that sharks are man-eaters.

The truth is, sharks aren't all that interested in humans. In lab tests involving small sharks, the species studied had a much greater interest in squid and shrimp blood versus human blood. Statistics provide corroboration.

The Global Shark Attack File is a comprehensive, public-access spreadsheet listing every recorded shark incident from 725 BCE to the present. According to the log, shark attacks on humans are rare. In 2019, for example, there were 57 documented shark/human encounters in US waters. Three involved great white sharks (or, more simply, white sharks), but none of those confrontations were fatal. In the log, only one incident from 2019 was listed as fatal, but scientists suspect the event was actually an accidental drowning that a shark used to its advantage. The following year, in 2020, three shark-related fatalities were documented off American shores.

Figures from the Australian Institute of Marine Science indicate that an average of 10 deaths attributable to shark attacks occur worldwide each year, compared to 150 average annual deaths caused by falling coconuts. By contrast, data from the National Safety Council show that 38,800 Americans died in car crashes in 2019, and that figure actually reveals a slight decrease in deaths from previous years, which the organization credits to several risk mitigation actions.

But using statistics to communicate danger is usually a lost cause. That's because we humans are crazy-bad at evaluating risk. Despite the figures on sharks and cars, we rarely think twice about jumping into an automobile, yet we irrationally fear oceanic predators.

"Evolutionarily, we have evolved to stay away from predators," Graham points out. But there's more to it than that, she says, because orcas and whales are also predators, and we humans aren't universally afraid of these massive mammals.

"Fearing sharks is reasonable because fear is a response we have developed throughout human evolution to protect ourselves," explains clinical psychologist Sara Knickerbocker, PhD, noting, "Fear overriding logic is what has led to a pervasive embrace of galeophobia [fear of sharks]." Inside our mortal brains, emotion takes the wheel, and logic takes a back seat.

Maybe the shark-car phenomenon can be chalked up to typical human psychology. It's not so unusual for people to underestimate large, ongoing dangers like car accidents, and obsess instead over small but scary risks (hello, sharks). In fact, current research indicates that our perception of risk is greatly influenced by two things: control and familiarity.

While driving your car to the beach might be riskier than swimming with a shark, when you're at the wheel you sure *feel* like you're in full control, even if the presence of other drivers means you aren't. As an example of familiarity, most of us interact with automobiles on a daily basis, but few people will see sharks up close during their lifetimes.

"The notion of instructional acquisition of fears explains why myths about sharks are so persistent," Knickerbocker adds. "This theory posits that the information we are given, or the reactions we observe, teach us what to be afraid of, even in the absence of direct experience," she says.

Risk and emotion can become hopelessly intertwined, and nobody understands that better than Hollywood writers and producers! "We learn that sharks should be feared, even in the absence of direct experience," Knickerbocker says. Who can forget that moment in *Jaws* when Hooper pulled Mr. Vaughan aside and said, "What we are dealing with here is a perfect engine—an eating machine"? It's no wonder the saying of the time was, "A good shark is a dead shark."

"The great white shark has such a bad reputation as a man eater that it's enough to make your skin crawl!" wrote Maud Fontenoy in a foreword to the book *Great White Shark: Myth and Reality.*

Forget fiction: "Pick up almost any book written about sharks in the 1950s or 60s, and you'll find myths printed all over the pages," Levine says. Even documentaries from the era—*The Silent World* (1956), for example, directed by renowned explorer Jacques-Yves Cousteau—characterized sharks as brute monsters.

And while missionaries and explorers had been comparing sharks to demons since the seventeenth century, America's shark phobia didn't really reach its zenith until 1974, when Peter Benchley released his book and screenplay for *Jaws.* A year later, Steven Spielberg turned *Jaws* into a blockbuster man-versus-shark horror movie, solidifying the great white's role as a savage.

Benchley, who passed away in 2006, lived only a few blocks from the Shark Research Institute, and here's one shark rumor that's really true: After seeing his work spark an international hysteria, Benchley dedicated the rest of his career to shark conservation and education.

"He became one of our strongest supporters," Levine recalls, adding, "Peter was surprised how many people took his book as factual, even though they bought it in the fiction section of the bookstore."

But then again, it's hard to know what's fact and fiction when an animal has largely evaded human observation. The world under the sea is almost alien-like compared to life on dry land, and when *Jaws* came out, marine biologists really didn't know much about sharks. Decades later, we've learned a lot more about sharks through comprehensive "tagging" programs that use radio transmitters to follow sharks.

Yet, scientists are still baffled by some shark behavior. Marine biologists, for example, didn't realize until the 1980s that female white sharks give birth to live young, and we still don't know the exact gestation period for whites.

Given these scientific gaps, it is no wonder public awareness of sharks has been limited. "One benefit of the book and movie is that it spurred considerable research on sharks," Levine says.

Starting with the basics, sharks aren't mammals like dolphins, whales, sea lions, otters, and so on. They're a group of fish lacking swim bladders, commonly recognized by the paired pectoral fins near their head, as well as a general propensity to lurk menacingly just below the water's surface.

Sharks really aren't trying to put off a bad vibe when they swim. "They don't have bones," Levine explains. "Their skeletons are made of cartilage," she continues, just like human noses. That's why they are so supple and glide smoothly through water. "They're not lurking. They're just swimming gracefully," Levine summarizes.

Over 500 species of shark populate the planet's oceans, ranging in size from teeny, 6-inch-long dwarf dogsharks to the gigantic whale shark, the largest fish in the world. And then there are great whites (*Carcharodon carcharias*). Nicknamed "white death," these large, formidable fish get all the hype.

When it comes to great whites, "people-eating is still a huge misconception," Levine notes, but because shark attacks generate attention-grabbing headlines, the news media continues to perpetuate the myth that sharks eat people. "Some accidents in which the only injury sustained was a cut to a person's toe have gone viral worldwide on the Internet," Levine says. In January 1905, for example, when a diver and a white shark collided in Buffels Bay, Cape Province, South Africa, newspapers portrayed the incident as an attack, even though the victim needed only a single Band-Aid™ to treat his injury.

Sharks could definitely use their teeth to bite a person—that's obviously true—but they aren't going to chew you up and eat you. Sharks can't chew their food because their jaws don't move side-to-side. (They only go up and down.) And what's more, Levine says, "Their stomachs really aren't large enough to hold an entire human." Graham adds, "A whale shark's esophagus is only a few inches in diameter, so they couldn't gobble us if they tried."

When it comes to people-eating, though, evolution is a much bigger hurdle to overcome than physiology. Sharks are truly primordial. They evolved 450 million years before humans arrived on the planet. They even predate dinosaurs by approximately 230 million years. "People just aren't on their menu," Levine explains.

Most species have specific diets. As an example, Levine points out that "we humans may eat salad greens, but we don't eat trees for dinner or harvest our lawns for snacks." The same

"Like all animals, sharks learn by exploring the environment," Levine says. Since they don't have hands, sharks use their nose, mouth, and teeth to examine new things, which could explain why many great white bites appear to involve juvenile sharks.

In 2000, an underwater cameraman was videotaping sharks in South African waters, examining how they approach humans, when a great white bit a diver's flipper. The entire underwater encounter was caught on film, and Levine and a colleague from the Shark Research Institute used the footage, along with bite patterns from that incident, and several others, to gain a better understanding of shark behavior and motivation.

"The videotaped incident showed that the shark's intention was not to bite through the fin or hold on to it," the researchers wrote in their paper *Use of Forensic Analysis to Better Understand Shark Attack Behaviour.* The observation confirms a scientific theory that white sharks often "grasp an object as an exploratory bite . . . to determine palatability."

Sharks have fine-tuned, efficient senses. Great whites, like other sharks, are equipped with an impressive assortment of first-rate sensory organs. There's the lateral line, for example, a set of pores running from snout to tail, used to detect vibrations from both prey and predators.

Even so, it is a myth that sharks can smell one drop of blood from miles away.

"Sharks are often portrayed as having an almost supernatural sense of smell," Levine says. Their olfactory systems are very sensitive, and yet reports that sharks can smell a single drop of blood in the ocean are "greatly exaggerated," Levine adds.

"This is a very common misconception," Graham says, offering, "In terms of smell, shark noses work a lot like our own human noses." In water, as in air, a smell is only detected if it actually reaches a set of nostrils. "You know when you're in a big room and somebody passes gas, and then there's a wave of people making funny faces?" she asks. If the room's big enough, and you're on the opposite end from where the smell originated, then you can breathe a sigh of relief because the smell probably won't get to you.

Hollywood producers might create the illusion that one drop of blood in the water can draw in sharks from across the globe. But back in the real world, Graham explains, "The ocean is a big, deep place," and smells will naturally dissipate in the water.

That said, the membranes inside a shark's nose are sensitive, and some sharks are able to detect miniscule amounts of certain chemicals. "This varies, of course, among different species of sharks and the chemical in question," Levine points out. The lemon shark, for example, can detect tuna oil at one part per 25 million. "That's equivalent to about 10 drops in an average-sized home swimming pool," says Levine, adding, "Other types of sharks can detect their prey at one part per 10 billion, or one drop in an Olympic-sized swimming pool."

While some shark species can detect blood at one part per million, Levine says, "That hardly qualifies as the entire ocean." Plus there are other factors to consider with oceanic scents, such as the speed and direction of the water current.

It's definitely a myth that menstruating women are more likely to be attacked by sharks.

A shark's sense of smell is impressive, but there's no evidence that menstrual blood attracts sharks. Women don't have to avoid the ocean during their time of the month.

"As I recall, the myth that sharks are attracted to menstrual blood was found to be false in the 1960s as a result of tests conducted in Hawaii by Dr. Albert Tester," Levine says. When a female is bitten, case investigators from the Shark

Research Institute routinely ask if she was menstruating, and the answer is often, "No."

What's more, Levine isn't totally convinced that sharks are drawn to blood at all. "When I've attempted to bring sharks close in order to tag them, it seems to me that it's not fish blood, but the visceral fluid of fish that brings the sharks close," she says, adding, "This makes sense because visceral fluid is lost when a fish is mortally injured."

One common misconception is that sharks only swim in salt water.

In reality, sharks can be found in every ocean on the planet, from tropical waters to Arctic and Antarctic regions. Bull sharks, for example, live in both salt- and freshwater, and they have been caught 2,294 miles up the Amazon River in Peru and 700 miles up the Mississippi River. Lake Nicaragua even has a landlocked population of bull sharks.

"There are sharks besides bull sharks that can go into freshwater," Graham says, pointing to lemon sharks and black-tips. Juveniles within these species are often found in brackish water, which is a term used to describe water that's saltier than freshwater but less saline than a true ocean (think: an estuary where the river and sea meet).

If that last paragraph made your skin crawl, keep in mind that we need sharks in the environment. "They are critical in maintaining a healthy and balanced ocean ecosystem," Levine explains, mainly by controlling and regulating the species below them in the food chain. In some areas where sharks have been removed, Levine says, "A trophic [or nutritional] cascade resulted."

In New Jersey, near the Shark Research Institute, many shark species fed on cownose rays, a species of eagle ray. When too many sharks were removed by overfishing, the area's population of cownose rays exploded. "Those thousands of rays fed on shellfish, ultimately decimating the local shellfish industry," Levine explains.

The last myth to bust is the misconception that great whites have no mortal enemies.

While orcas (i.e., killer whales) and some larger shark species sometimes prey on white sharks, the animal's main predators are humans. "We're more dangerous to sharks than they are to us," Levine says. Humans kill 73 million to 100 million sharks each year.

Shark meat contains many toxins, from methylmercury and polychlorinated biphenyls to DDT, a colorless, tasteless, and almost odorless crystalline chemical compound. On top of that, the meat spoils lightning-quick due to its high content of urea. The only usable part of a shark is its fins, so most sharks, then, are killed solely for their fins. "Finning is the practice in which shark fins are sliced off and the shark is thrown back into the ocean, usually alive," Levine explains, adding, "Unable to swim, and bleeding profusely, the shark either suffocates or dies of blood loss."

Shark fins can be used in shark fin soup. The soup is either pork or chicken broth with a bit of cartilage from a fin thrown in. "The cartilage has no nutritional value and adds no taste," Levine notes. Priced at $100 to $150 a bowl, ordering shark fin soup is a status symbol in some countries.

Some shark species, including white sharks and other pelagics, don't do well in public aquariums. In the wild, they roam huge distances, but when kept inside an aquarium tank, they tend to ram into walls and injure themselves. "White sharks in captivity have lived only a few days or weeks, and whale sharks in aquariums in Japan and the US have a far shorter lifespan than they do in the wild," says Levine. So if you're going to an aquarium, or doing an eco-tourism dive trip, make sure the organization you're patronizing is really considering the health and safety of sharks and tourists alike.

If you're still nervous about sharing the water with sharks, the Shark Research Institute provides practical ways to lower your odds of a rare encounter. First and foremost, always check local reports before swimming, especially in areas where shark attacks have previously occurred.

Be aware of your surroundings, and take note of the behavior of marine life nearby. If a pod of dolphins is breaching nearby, that could mean sharks are feeding in the area. Dolphins often follow sharks to capitalize on their leftovers.

If you're really into dotting your *I*s, don't buy a swimsuit with contrasting colors such as black and white for your ocean adventures. The jury's still out, but many scientists think sharks might be attracted to high-contrast colors. That's why experts at the Florida Museum recommend wearing dark blue or black swimwear and dive gear. It's also smart to refrain from excess splashing and abrupt movements since that's exactly what sea animals do when they're in distress.

If you do see a shark while swimming or diving, don't touch it, even if it's small, because any shark is capable of injuring you. Avoid swimming in murky water, and experts warn against nighttime dips because evidence indicates sharks move in closer to land once the sun sets. Since sharks might be more likely to bite solo swimmers and divers, experts also recommend recreating with a partner or in a group. Plus, if you're injured while alone, it'll be that much harder to get help.

If you're bitten, and you're wearing a wetsuit, don't remove the wetsuit unless it's necessary to control bleeding from an artery. Generally speaking, your wetsuit will act as a pressure bandage, restricting blood loss until help arrives.

Many shark fatalities recorded in the Global Shark Attack File could have been avoided if arterial bleeding had been recognized and stopped, and basic life support provided. Take both a CPR course and an advanced first-aid course. Gut instincts should also be heeded: If you suddenly become uneasy, leave the water immediately.

BOTTOM LINE: Sharks certainly have enough physical prowess to harm swimmers and divers, and yet shark-human encounters remain rare. Sharks aren't man-eaters. While shark attacks definitely make for attention-grabbing headlines and blockbuster movies, the truth is that humans aren't on the menu for these primordial creatures.

The New Rule on Bear Safety

Hiking alongside abundant salmon streams such as McNeil River on the remote Alaska Peninsula, surrounded by feeding bears, one fact is clear: "Bears here generally don't care about humans one way or another," says John Hechtel, a retired wildlife biologist for Alaska's Department of Fish and Game (ADF&G).

"The people most familiar with bears tend to be the least afraid," Hechtel continues. During his 30-year tenure with ADF&G, he introduced hundreds of skittish visitors to wild bears. Hechtel describes one conflicted visitor from the East Coast who was simultaneously drawn to McNeil River to see bears and also frightened at the thought of camping in such a wild area. Watching this particular tourist learn to trust the guides, begin to understand bears, and overcome his fear— that's what turned Hechtel into an advocate for bear-viewing programs.

Bears fascinate people. And let's be honest, most of us really enjoy hearing scary stories about bear attacks. A good yarn over the campfire can be fun, but tales of maulings do more to frighten listeners than help people understand bears.

That's problematic: "When inexperienced people encounter a bear, even in nonthreatening situations, many panic," explains Hechtel, and that's when an otherwise benign scenario can take a turn for the worst.

North America provides habitat for three of the world's eight bear species: polar, black, and brown (commonly called grizzlies). Polar bears are easiest for amateurs to identify given their light fur color. Laypeople, however, often struggle to distinguish between black and brown bears. "Many people are confused by the bears' common names," Hechtel explains.

"Black" and "brown" aren't fur colors. They're species.

Color is not a reliable method for differentiating black and brown bears. In fact, American black bears (*Ursus americanus*) come in a wide variety of colors. "The brown color phase of American black bears in California and Colorado, for example, are commonly called brown bears, which is also a name for grizzly bears (*Ursus arctos*) in places like Coastal Alaska," Hechtel says, adding that "the bears many people call 'grizzlies' in North America are called brown bears in other places around the world."

Confused yet? This discrepancy is one of the primary reasons biologists prefer to use scientific names. Latin terminology might be harder to pronounce, but it is consistent and won't vary by region. For the sake of clarity, in this chapter we'll use the terms "black bear" for *Ursus americanus* and "grizzly" when referring to *Ursus arctos*.

A few physical differences can help nonbiologists distinguish between black bears and grizzlies. According to the North American Bear Center, grizzlies tend to be larger than black bears, and they also have more prominent shoulder humps and tend to have a more dish-shaped face profile.

Grizzlies also have longer, blunter claws than black bears. This feature is an adaptation for securing food: In the open habitats where many grizzlies evolved, the species developed claws that could dig up roots and burrowing animals. Meanwhile, black bears that inhabit forested areas needed shorter, curved claws useful for climbing trees when evading predators.

Physical differences aside, black bears and grizzlies have a lot in common, and in many ways, they're the humans of the forest and tundra—intelligent, opportunistic omnivores. All bears have large brains relative to their body size. In fact, they're considered to be one of the world's smartest animals. They're expert navigators with outstanding long-term memories. "Bears may travel long distances knowing where and when to show up for seasonal feeding opportunities like salmon runs on the Alaskan Coast," Hechtel says.

Bears have remarkable olfactory systems. "According to new research, a bear's sense of smell has been calculated to be roughly 2,000 times better than a human's," says Ben Lawhon, senior director of research and consulting for the Leave No Trace Center for Outdoor Ethics. (This is why it's so important for campers to properly store their food, trash, and "smelly" items, including toothpaste and lip balm.)

Bears are solitary animals, but they aren't antisocial by any means. Just like people, bears have a social structure with a handful of rules. While the term "alpha" might be a misnomer for wolves (see "Wolves, Explained"), the principle definitely pertains to bears, which employ a pecking order to share resources and get along with one another.

"Their main concern is food," Hechtel points out. In a forest, where food might be scarce, bears tend to keep to themselves. But when there's a salmon stream flush with thousands of fish, they'll mingle. It wouldn't make any sense for a bear to try to protect an abundant food source. "Bears simply take turns," says Hechtel, explaining that "the dominant bear chooses the best feeding spot, goes first, feeds, and then moves away so less dominant bears can then feed."

"If bears don't know where another bear or a person falls in the pecking order, they tend to respond based on the bear's or the human's behavior," Hechtel continues.

If you live or recreate in bear country, which extends from Everglades National Park in south Florida, all the way up to the Alaskan frontier, then you've probably heard the hackneyed recommendation to always play dead during a grizzly attack and fight back against a black bear.

It's a common myth that bear species should determine how outdoors enthusiasts respond to bear encounters.

The play-dead/fight-back fallacy arose because early studies indicated there were two totally different types of bear attacks (defensive and aggressive) that required different responses. The data used for these studies suggested that grizzly bears usually only attacked when provoked and were just trying to defend themselves, their cubs, or a food cache. Defensive black bear attacks were thought to be rare. So in the 1900s, wildlife managers designed safety campaigns that encouraged outdoors enthusiasts to respond to bears based on the species they encountered. "This was a simple way to teach people how to react rather than trying to explain bear behavior," says Hechtel.

The problem is that bear behavior is anything but simple. (Remember, bears are a lot like us humans!) "Everyone wants one simple answer for what do I do if a bear approaches," Hechtel adds. In reality, a simple solution doesn't exist.

Let's start by exploring the rationale behind the play-dead with grizzlies, fight-back with black bears advice.

After being killed off in much of their range by the early 1900s, fewer than 2,000 grizzly bears remain in the lower 48 states. This wasn't always the case. At one point in history, grizzlies roamed most of the country west of the Mississippi. While some dwelled in massive, old-growth forests, the majority lived in areas lacking trees: grasslands, prairie, lowlands, and tundra.

"Grizzlies evolved in open habitats, where there were other large predators such as saber tooth tigers, and the theory is that without effective escape cover, they had to evolve to be more aggressive to protect themselves and their offspring," Hechtel explains. Black bears, on the other hand, evolved in forested areas, where mother bears could escape with their cubs into the trees.

For years biologists and rangers perpetuated the play-dead/fight-back directive by telling recreationists that grizzly bears were the only bears that will attack to defend their cubs. Experts now know that, though it is less common, some black bears will also aggressively defend their cubs. And conversely, they've documented incidences of grizzlies attacking nondefensively, while seeking human food or even acting as predators (two scenarios when playing dead is a bad idea).

So while the theory surrounding species-based play-dead/fight-back advice seemed to make sense for the most common serious attacks, this quick tip for navigating bear encounters is incorrect and "way too simplistic," as Hechtel puts it.

Both species of bears (black and grizzly) can display two types of aggression: defensive and nondefensive, the latter of which is also called "offensive" by some biologists. In the rare event of an aggressive bear encounter, the reason for the bear's aggression is more important than the species of bear. "The advice should be to play dead if a bear attack is defensive, and fight back if it's not," Hechtel clarifies. Outdoors enthusiasts can use context clues to discern a bear's motivation, and we'll get into that in a moment. First, though, let's look at the two types of aggression.

Defensive aggression arises when humans fail to understand and respect a bear's sense of social norms. You know when you're at the office holiday party and a coworker swoops in from out of nowhere, leans too close, and starts talking to you, blowing their hot breath all over your face? In this scenario, most of us will feel crowded and more than a little bit uncomfortable. Just like us, bears are sensitive to unexpected and unwanted invasions of personal space. Only, a bear's comfort zone is quite a bit larger than yours!

It's a myth that bears are territorial.

Scientifically speaking, a territory is an area an animal defends. "Bears don't defend the area where they live," Hechtel notes. Rather, bears have "zones," which are basically these individual bubbles of personal space that follow the bear as it moves through the wild. And sometimes, bears will react aggressively in defense of that personal space.

While most people like to maintain a distance of 2 or 3 feet from others, bears need more room. They might feel crowded even at 50 yards. "This is just one of the cultural differences between humans and bears," explains Hechtel. As long as you're respecting a bear's need for space, an encounter should be benign.

"If someone starts to encroach on the edge of a bear's zone, the bear will start to pay attention," Hechtel says. And if you happen to startle a black bear or grizzly when you're well within their personal space . . . that's when the bear's fight or flight response is triggered. Defensive aggression occurs when a bear believes a human poses a threat—especially a mother and her cubs or a bruin on a carcass. Hence, experts often refer to defensive attacks as "provoked" because human behavior triggered the attack.

But to complicate matters, there are times when bears will exhibit nondefensive (i.e., offensive) aggression—like when a bear raids a campsite. In nondefensive scenarios, the bear is the one that approaches people, or their campsites or dwellings, typically in search of food. "These bears are often calm and focused and bold," Hechtel says. And while it's hard to talk about predation without reinforcing excessive bear fear, it's true that *some bears* will even prey on people in rare instances. This is another form of offensive aggression.

According to "Fatal Attacks by American Black Bear on People," a research report published in the *Journal of Wildlife Management* in 2011, black bears killed 63 people in North America over the 109-year period between 1900 and 2009. Researchers have determined that at least 88 percent of the attacks were predatory, meaning the bears involved treated their victims as prey. But putting that into perspective, there are many hundreds of thousands of black bears living in close proximity to people throughout much of North America. Predatory attacks are extremely unlikely.

Bears evolved as omnivores with a varied diet of roots, berries, acorns, nuts, fruit, and insects, as well as succulent greens including shoots and grasses. "You can see a bunch of bears grazing like cows in sedge meadows in Alaska," says Hechtel, describing bears as "supreme opportunists when it comes to food." Bears love fresh, wild-caught salmon, and they'll also eat moose and deer flesh.

Repeat after me: The vast majority of wild bears don't want to eat humans. (If they did, there'd be a lot more attacks.) "A bear could get hurt in a confrontation with a human, and it doesn't want that," Hechtel points out. For bears, he continues, "The name of the game is consuming the most calories they can get for the amount of effort they have to put in." After all, many bears have as little as six months to ingest all the calories they'll need for the year. "They eat like crazy, then live off extra fat during hibernation. That's their lifestyle," says Hechtel.

Many of the most serious black bear attacks have been predatory, and many minor bites and swats are related to food seeking. This further explains how experts came up with the advice to always fight back against a black bear. But recent studies have documented black bears defensively attacking to protect cubs; other times, domesticated dogs have provoked black bears.

Your response to a bear attack should depend on the individual bear's motivation.

In the very rare event that a bear charges at you—and this really is rare—your best bet is to use context clues to *quickly* determine why, exactly, the bear is approaching.

Let's say you're trekking through a forested area, and you're slacking off, not making enough noise. You come around a corner. All of a sudden there's a big bear. Maybe the bear's near a secret food source or has a cub nearby. Before you know what's happening, the bruin is charging. Oftentimes, defensive bears will rush forward, retreat, and then rush forward again, repeating their charge several times.

The bear was caught off guard, and it is exhibiting classic signs of defensive aggression, using body language to tell you to "stand down." In this situation, you should try to stand your ground, stay calm, and talk in a low soothing voice, which lets the bear know you're not a threat. Preferably you're doing this while holding a can of bear spray, just in case.

The bear isn't trying to be a tough guy. It feels scared and is responding to its fight-or-flight impulses. Often by giving the bear information and time to determine that you aren't dangerous, the situation will be safely resolved. However, "If you don't have bear spray, and a defensive bear knocks you to the ground, then the best thing is to keep still," Hechtel says. This course of action communicates to the bear that you aren't a threat.

The advice is the exact opposite for those who encounter bears showing offensive aggression. If a bear calmly walks toward your picnic table, or you're out hiking and a bear casually meanders toward you, you'll want to communicate to the bear that you're much bigger and stronger than you seem. "Bears are usually cautious," Hechtel says, "because it's risky for them if they pick a fight with an animal that can do them harm."

When a bear's not upset—not freaking out—that's your cue that it is curious, looking for handouts, or possibly predatory. In this scenario, do your best to stay calm, talk sternly, and bang pots and pans if you've got them. Throw stones, too, if you can reach them without making yourself look small by bending down. The bear will probably wander off. If you're mauled, fight back, and always protect your head and neck.

It's a misconception that bears are more likely to attack when they lose their fear of people.

"A lot of people use 'habituation' as a synonym for 'food conditioned,'" Hechtel says, adding, "We've tried to correct this language, but sometimes even park rangers still get confused."

The terms "habituation" and "food conditioned" represent two completely different ideas. Habituation happens when an animal is exposed to a certain stimulus over and over again, with no consequences. Eventually, the animal grows so accustomed to something that it simply stops paying attention.

New Yorkers, for example, are so used to traffic sirens that they can sleep right through them. Similarly, in popular outdoor recreation areas, especially state and national parks, some bears become so acclimated to people that they stop paying attention and ignore most human behavior.

Some people believe that if a bear doesn't flee from humans, something is wrong, but that's not necessarily true. Habituated bears don't run from people, nor do they seek them out. As such, habituation is neither good nor bad. "It is a state of being neutral," Hechtel explains. And at bear-viewing areas such as McNeil River or Brooks Camp in Katmai, habituated bears that have never gotten food or garbage from people present amazing opportunities for viewers to photograph bears going about their lives as if people weren't around.

A lot of people, though, misuse the term "habituation." Bears and other animals don't "habituate" to garbage. Rather, they can become "food conditioned" when they get a yummy reward for raiding a trash can, campground, or bird feeder.

Food conditioned bears can become attracted to the places where people live or camp. (Free food! Why not?)

"Habituation itself isn't a problem," Hechtel reiterates. But habituation can lead to conflicts. If humans see bears that aren't avoiding people, they may try to approach such bears, and this human behavior can trigger a defensive response. Or if people are careless with food and garbage in areas habituated bears frequent, then trouble can definitely arise as a bear becomes habituated *and* food conditioned. When this happens, bears can start to become aggressive in pursuit of food, even breaking into buildings and vehicles. They can also get seriously injured messing around in trash receptacles and other unsafe places, but such bears usually end up being killed. For everybody's sake, be sure to store your food properly while camping and picnicking, and never feed wild animals.

Bears are not homicidal killers. They aren't larger-than-life stuffed animals either.

"Once people get to know bears, they start to realize they aren't waiting in the woods to kick our butts," Hechtel says. They are just trying to survive, live their lives, and reproduce.

Alaska claims the bulk of North America's grizzly population (35,000 bruins) plus over 100,000 black bears and up to 5,000 polar bears. In the last frontier, where bears roam freely, over the last 40 years the authorities have recorded about one fatal bear attack every 2 years. "We see six to seven attacks annually, and those are mostly with grizzlies," Hechtel adds.

Despite reassuring statistics, it's hard not to get clammy hands when hiking through a dense patch of forest in the heart of bear country. Some biologists have speculated that bear-related anxiety is primal. During evolution, before early humans had reliable weapons, bears were formidable animals. "There could be some stuff wired into our brains," says Hechtel, noting, "That's only a theory."

The media hasn't done much to dispel any innate fears we humans might have. If you read *Outdoor Life*, books of collected bear attack tales, or even your local newspaper, you've probably noticed "a very skewed picture of what bears are all about," adds Hechtel. The vast majority of the time, human-bear interactions are ordinary and uneventful. But few media outlets report on typical encounters involving a chance meeting that ends with the bear slinking back into the woods as the human slowly backtracks.

"Driving in your vehicle to a trailhead is more dangerous than a bear encounter," Hechtel points out. And yet many people are more concerned about animal attacks than auto accidents. (For more on the psychology behind this phenomenon, see chapter 12 on sharks.)

So don't be afraid to recreate in bear country, but don't underestimate wild bears either. Bears might not have murderous intentions, but they aren't giant animated toys. You don't want to get complacent because with a little effort, most conflicts with bears can be prevented. "Bears are large, potentially dangerous animals. We need to learn about how to reduce our risks, prevent problems and get in the habit of carrying a deterrent like bear spray. It's important to respect, not fear them, and act accordingly," says Hechtel.

BOTTOM LINE: It would be nice to have a simple rule of thumb to employ in the event of a bear encounter. But the outdated advice to "always play dead with a grizzly and fight back with a black bear" is incorrect. If you spend a lot of time in the woods, the safest thing to do is carry a chest holster with bear spray on it. Learn how bears view social situations, and be prepared by knowing how you'll react to the two types of aggression. Whatever you do, don't let anxiety about bears interfere with your enjoyment of the great outdoors.

Bibliography

Abromeit, Doug. "United States Military Artillery for Avalanche Control Program: A Short History in Time." *Alaska Department of Transportation and Public Facilities.* www.dot.alaska.gov/stwd .mno/documents/History_Military_Weapons_Avalanche.pdf.

Achenbach, Joel. 2011. "Zoo Mystery: How Did Apes and Birds Know Quake Was Coming?" Health and Science. *Washington Post.* August 24. www.washingtonpost.com/national/health -science/zoo-mystery-how-did-apes-and-birds-know-quake -was-coming/2011/08/24/gIQAZrXQcJ_story.html.

American Meteorological Society. "Thunderstorm Charge Separation." *American Meteorological Society.* Last Updated April 25, 2012. Accessed November 9, 2021. https://glossary.ametsoc .org/wiki/Thunderstorm_charge_separation.

Australian Department of Agriculture, Water and the Environment. "Sharks in Australian Waters." Last updated October 15, 2021. Accessed November 12, 2021. www.awe.gov.au/environment /marine/marine-species/sharks.

Ba, Djibril M., Paddy Ssentongo, Robert B. Beelman, Joshua Muscat, Xiang Gao, John P. Richie, Jr. 2021. "Higher Mushroom Consumption Is Associated with Lower Risk of Cancer: A Systematic Review and Meta-Analysis of Observational Studies." *Advances in Nutrition* 12, no. 5 (September): 1691–1704. doi.org/10.1093/advances/nmab015.

Battaglin, William A., Paul M. Bradley, Luke Iwanowicz, Celeste A. Journey, Heather L. Walsh, Vicki S. Blazer. 2018. "Pharmaceuticals, Hormones, Pesticides, and Other Bioactive Contaminants in Water, Sediment, and Tissue from Rocky Mountain National Park, 2012–2013." *Science of the Total Environment.* Vol. 643 (December): 651–73.

BBC. 2015. "Constipated Girl Emily Titterington from Cornwall Died Because Care Was Resisted." Cornwall. July 2. www.bbc .com/news/uk-england-cornwall-33357284.

Blackwell, Meredith. 2011. "The Fungi: 1, 2, 3 . . . 5.1 Million Species?" *Am. J Bot.* 98(3) (March): 426–38. DOI: 10.3732 /ajb.1000298.

Beug, Michael. 2021. *Mushrooms of Cascadia: An Illustrated Key.* Batavia, IL: The FUNGI Press.

Bradbury, John. 1904. *Travels in the Interior of America: In the Years 1809, 1810, and 1811.* Edited by Reuben Gold Thwaites. Volume 5 of Early Western Travels. Chicago: The Arthur H. Clark Company.

California State University San Marcos. "Earthquake Myths and Facts: Earthquake Mythology or . . . Don't Believe Everything You Hear!" *California State University San Marcos.* Accessed November 9, 2021. www.csusm.edu/em/procedures/earthquake _myths.html.

Centers for Disease Control and Prevention. "Lightning: Victim Data." *Centers for Disease Control and Prevention.* Last reviewed December 23, 2013. Accessed November 9, 2021. www.cdc.gov /disasters/lightning/victimdata.html.

Civard-Racinais, Alexandrine. 2012. *Great White Sharks: Myth and Reality.* Buffalo: Firefly Books.

Clark, Liesl. 2000. "Polynesia's Genius Navigators." Ancient Worlds. *Rocky Mountain PBS.* February 14. www.pbs.org/wgbh/nova /article/polynesia-genius-navigators.

Clements, Deborah S. "Quick Dose: Why Does the Cold Weather Make My Nose Run?" *Northwestern Medicine.* Accessed November 8, 2021. www.nm.org/healthbeat/healthy-tips /why-does-the-cold-weather-make-my-nose-run.

Colorado Avalanche Information Center. 2021. "Statistics and Reporting." *Colorado Avalanche Information Center.* www .avalanche.state.co.us/accidents/statistics-and-reporting/.

Davies, Mary Ann. 2004. "What's Burning in Your Campfire? Garbage In, Toxins Out." *Recreation Tech Tips*. *USDA Forest Service*. September. https://eec.ky.gov/Environmental -Protection/Air/Documents/WhatsBurninginYourCampfire _Article.pdf.

Densmore, Lisa. 2010. *Predicting Weather: Forecasting, Planning and Preparing*. Lanham, MD: Falcon Guides.

Fantastic Fungi. 2019. Directed by Louis Schwartzberg. Narrated by Brie Larson. Moving Art. Netflix.

Foxman, Ellen F., James A. Storer, Megan E. Fitzgerald, Bethany R. Wasik, Lin Hou, Hongyu Zhao, Paul E. Turner, Anna Marie Pyle, Akiko Iwasaki. 2015. "Temperature-Dependent Innate Control of Rhinovirus." *Proceedings of the National Academy of Sciences* 112 (3) 827–32 (January). DOI: 10.1073 /pnas.1411030112.

Friedman, John. 2009. *Out of the Blue: A History of Lightning: Science, Superstition, and Amazing Stories of Survival*. London: Delta.

Gilbert, Mads, Rolf Busund, Arne Skagseth, Paul Åge Nilsen, Jan P. Solbø. 2000. "Resuscitation from Accidental Hypothermia of 13·7°C with Circulatory Arrest." *The Lancet*, vol. 335:9201 (375–763). January 29. DOI: doi.org/10.1016 /S0140-6736(00)01021-7.

Glime, J. M. 2017. *Meet the Bryophytes*. Vol. 1. Chap. 2-1. Physiological Ecology. Ebook. Sponsored by Michigan Technological University and the International Association of Bryologists. Last updated August 22, 2020. Accessed November 14, 2021. http://digitalcommons.mtu.edu/bryophyte-ecology.

Greenwood, Leigh. 2021. "Firewood as a Vector of Forest Pest Dispersal in North America: What Do We Know and What Do We Need to Know?" *DontMoveFirewood.org* (blog). January 28. www.dontmovefirewood.org/firewood-as-a-vector-of-forest -pest-dispersal-in-north-america-what-do-we-know-and-what -do-we-need-to-know.

Hough, Susan E. 2018. "Do Large Magnitude Global Earthquakes Occur on Preferred Days of the Calendar Year or Lunar Cycle?" *Seismological Research Letters* 89 (2A): 577–81. DOI: https://doi .org/10.1785/0220170154.

International Wolf Center. "Types of Wolves." *International Wolf Center.* Accessed November 9, 2021. https://wolf.org/wolf-info /basic-wolf-info/types-of-wolves.

Janský, L., D. Pospísilová, S. Honzová, B. Ulicný, P. Srámek, V. Zeman, J. Kamínková. 1996. "Immune System of Cold-Exposed and Cold-Adapted Humans." *Eur J Appl Physiol Occup Physiol* 72 (5-6): 445–50. DOI: 10.1007/BF00242274.

Johnson, Daniel. 2018. "Meet Polaris, the North Star." Night Sky Sights. *Sky and Telescope,* April 19. https://skyandtelescope.org /astronomy-news/meet-polaris-the-north-star.

Jones, A. Raymond. 1998. "Hipparchus," *Encyclopedia Britannica.* Last modified June 15, 2021. www.britannica.com/biography /Hipparchus-Greek-astronomer.

Kendrick, Bryce. 2017. *The Fifth Kingdom: An Introduction to Mycology.* 4th ed. Indianapolis/Cambridge, MA: Hackett Publishing Company.

Living with Wolves. "Tackling the Myths." *Living with Wolves.* Accessed November 9, 2021. www.livingwithwolves.org /about-wolves/tackling-the-myths.

Mapes, Lynda V. 2010. "1910 Stevens Pass Avalanche Still Deadliest in U.S. History." Local News. *Seattle Times.* February 27. www .seattletimes.com/seattle-news/1910-stevens-pass-avalanche -still-deadliest-in-us-history/.

Marrone, Teresa, and Kathy Yerich. *Mushrooms of the Upper Midwest: A Simple Guide to Common Mushrooms.* Vol. 2. Cambridge, MN: Adventure Publications.

Martin, Annie. 2015. *The Magical World of Moss Gardening.* Portland, OR: Timber Press.

McClure, Bruce. 2019. "Brightest Stars: Polaris is the North Star." *Earth Sky*. Last modified May 21. https://earthsky.org /brightest-stars/polaris-the-present-day-north-star.

McEwen, Annie, and Brenna Farrell. 2016. "From Tree to Shining Tree." Produced by WNYC. *Radio Lab*. July 30. Podcast, 34:46. www.wnycstudios.org/podcasts/radiolab/articles /from-tree-to-shining-tree.

Mech, L. David. 1981. *The Wolf: The Ecology and Behavior of an Endangered Species*. Minneapolis: University of Minnesota Press.

Moore, David. 1999. "Fungus." *Encyclopedia Britannica*. Last modified Feb. 27, 2020. www.britannica.com/science/fungus.

National Interagency Fire Center. "National Fire News." Fire Information. *National Interagency Fire Center*. Accessed November 12, 2021. www.nifc.gov/fire-information/nfn.

National Interagency Fire Center. "Statistics." Fire Information. *National Interagency Fire Center*. Accessed November 12, 2021. www.nifc.gov/fire-information/statistics.

National Oceanic and Atmospheric Administration. "Tsunami Awareness." *Ocean Today*. Accessed November 8, 2021. https:// oceantoday.noaa.gov/tsunami-awareness.

National Safety Council. 2021. "Protect Yourself and Loved Ones by Addressing Roadway Risks." *National Safety Council*. Accessed November 14, 2021. www.nsc.org/road-safety/safety-topics /fatality-estimates.

National Weather Service. "Introduction to Lightning." *National Oceanic and Atmospheric Administration*. Accessed November 9, 2021. www.weather.gov/jetstream/lightning_intro.

National Weather Service. "Lightning Science: Five Ways Lightning Strikes People." *National Oceanic and Atmospheric Administration*. Accessed November 9, 2021. www.weather.gov /safety/lightning-struck#:~:text=Whether%20inside%20or%20

outside%2C%20anyone,phones%2C%20and%20windows%20
and%20doors.

North American Bear Center. "How to Tell Black Bears
from Brown/Grizzly Bears." North American Bear
Center. Accessed December 20, 2021. https://bear.org
/how-to-tell-black-bears-from-browngrizzly-bears.

North American Mycological Association. "Mushroom Poisoning
Syndromes." *North American Mycological Association.* Accessed
November 12, 2021. https://namyco.org/mushroom_poisoning
_syndromes.php.

Nuttle, Otto W. 1974. "1811–1812 New Madrid Earthquakes
Overview." *United States Geological Survey.* March-April. www
.usgs.gov/natural-hazards/earthquake-hazards/science/1811
-1812-new madrid-earthquakes-overview-otto-w-nuttli?qt
-science_center_objects=0#qt-science_center_objects.

Outdoor Foundation. 2021. "2021 Special Report: The New
Outdoor Participant (Covid and Beyond)." *Outdoor Participation
Report.* Published by the Outdoor Industry Association. June.
https://outdoorindustry.org/oia-participation/.

Peterson, Brenda. 2017. "An Historic Rage." Chapter 1 in *Wolf
Nation: The Life, Death, and Return of Wild American Wolves.*
Boston: Da Capo Press.

Polozov, I., L. Bezrukov, K. Gawrisch, et al. 2008. "Progressive
Ordering with Decreasing Temperature of the Phospholipids
of Influenza Virus." *Nat Chem Biol* 4, 248–255. https://doi
.org/10.1038/nchembio.77.

Prudente, Tim. 2015. "Seeing Stars, Again: Naval Academy
Reinstates Celestial Navigation." Cyber Crime. *Capital Gazette.*
October 12. www.capitalgazette.com/ph-ac-cn-celestial-naviga
tion-1014-20151009-story.html.

Reuter, Benjamin, Jürg Schweizer. 2009. "Avalanche Triggering by
Sound: Myth and Truth." Presented at the International Snow
Science Workshop. http://gblanc.fr/IMG/pdf/reuter2009.pdf.

Ritter, E. M. Levine. 2004. "Use of Forensic Analysis to Better Understand Shark Attack Behaviour." *Journal of Forensic Odonto-Stomatology*. 22:2 (December). https://static1.square space.com/static/5bae466429f2cc29475d636e/t/5c74ad5c4e 17b619cc5aba12/1551150429029/Ritter-Levine-2004.pdf.

Ryan, Laura A., David J. Slip, Lucille Chapuis, Shaun P. Collin, Enrico Gennari, Jan M. Hemmi, Martin J. How, Charlie Huveneers, Victor M. Peddemors, Louise Tosetto, and Nathan S. Hart. 2021. "A Shark's Eye View: Testing the 'Mistaken Identity Theory' behind Shark Bites on Humans." *Journal of the Royal Society Interface* 18, 183 (October). https://royalsociety publishing.org/doi/10.1098/rsif.2021.0533.

Settles, G. S. 2006. "High-Speed Imaging of Shock Waves, Explosions and Gunshots." *American Scientist*, 94 (1), 22. www .americanscientist.org/article/high-speed-imaging-of-shock -waves-explosions-and-gunshots.

Shaman, J., V. E. Pitzer, C. Viboud, B. T. Grenfell, M. Lipsitch. 2010. "Absolute Humidity and the Seasonal Onset of Influenza in the Continental United States." *PLoS Biol* 8(2): e1000316. https:// doi.org/10.1371/journal.pbio.1000316.

Shark Research Institute. 1991–2015. "Global Shark Attack File." *Shark Research Institute*. Accessed November 10, 2021. www .sharkattackfile.net/.

Shark Research Institute. 2005. "Recommendations." *Global Shark Attack File*. Accessed November 9, 2021. www.sharkattackfile .net/recommendations.htm.

Sieh, Kerry. "M7.9 1857 Fort Tejon Earthquake." *U.S. Geological Survey*. Accessed November 10, 2021. www.usgs.gov/natural -hazards/earthquake-hazards/science/m79-1857-fort -tejon-earthquake?qt-science_center_objects=0#qt-science _center_objects.

SmokyMountains.com. "Safe and Found." *SmokyMountains.com*. Accessed November 9, 2021. https://smokymountains.com /safe-and-found.

Stevens, D., A. Hussmann. 2017. "Wildlife Poop versus Dog Poop: Explained." *Leave No Trace* (blog). https://lnt.org/blog/wildlife-poop-versus-dog-poop-explained.

Strieker, Gary. 1997. "Man-Eating Wolves Terrorize Indian Villages." *CNN.* July 22. http://edition.cnn.com/EARTH/9707/22/man.eating.wolves/index.html.

Terrill, Andrew. 2021. *The Earth Beneath My Feet: A 7,000-Mile Walk of Discovery into the Heart of Wild Nature.* Golden, CO: Enchanted Rock Press.

Thomas, Robert B. 2015. "Cosmic Misconceptions: Common Misunderstandings about Astronomy," pages 142–44 in *The Old Farmer's Almanac.* Dublin, NH: Yankee Publishing.

Trynoski, Stephen E., Janice M. Glime. 1982. "Direction and Height of Bryophytes on Four Species of Northern Trees." *Bryologist* 85 (3): 281–300. Autumn. www.jstor.org/stable/3243047.

Tumas, Austin. 2020. "Biological Soil Crust of Southeast Utah." *National Park Service.* Last updated February 15. www.nps.gov/articles/seug-soil-crust.htm.

USDA. 2019. "Wolf Damage and Conflict Management in Wyoming: Environmental Assessment." *USDA.* May. www.aphis.usda.gov/wildlife_damage/nepa/states/WY/wy-2019-gray-wolf-damage-and-conflict-mgt-ea.pdf.

US Department of Defense. 1957. "Chapter 15: Cold Weather Survival" in *US Army Field Manual: Survival, FM 21-76.* New York: Ravenio Books. www.survivalebooks.com/15.htm#par3.

US Geological Survey. "Cool Earthquake Facts." *U.S. Geological Survey.* Accessed November 10, 2021. www.usgs.gov/natural-hazards/earthquake-hazards/science/cool-earthquake-facts?qt-science_center_objects=0#qt-science_center_objects.

US Geological Survey. "Earthquake Facts and Earthquake Fantasy." *U.S. Geological Survey.* Accessed November 10, 2021. www.usgs.gov/natural-hazards/earthquake-hazards/science

/earthquake-facts-earthquake-fantasy?qt-science_center
_objects=0#qt-science_center_objects.

Vella, Chantal, A. Len Kravitz. 2004. "Staying Cool When Your
Body Is Hot." AWKA. January. www.unm.edu/~lkravitz
/Article%20folder/thermoregulation.html.

Vreeman, Rachel C., Aaron E. Carroll. 2008. "Festive Medical
Myths." BMJ 337:a2769. www.bmj.com/content/337/bmj
.a2769.

Wait, T. C. 2018. "What We Learned from Alaska's Point
Mackenzie Earthquake." *RV Life*. December 6. https://rvlife
.com/alaska-earthquake-2018.

West, Julie. "North Star to Freedom." *National Park Service*. Accessed
November 9, 2021. www.nps.gov/articles/drinkinggourd.htm.

Wielgus, R. B., K. A. Peebles. 2014. "Effects of Wolf Mortality on
Livestock Depredations." *PLoS ONE* 9 (12): e113505. https://
doi.org/10.1371/journal.pone.0113505.

The 10 Essentials

American Hiking Society recommends you pack the "Ten Essentials" every time you head out for a hike. Whether you plan to be gone for a couple of hours or several months, make sure to pack these items. Become familiar with these items and know how to use them.

1. Appropriate Footwear

Happy feet make for pleasant hiking. Think about traction, support, and protection when selecting well-fitting shoes or boots.

2. Navigation

While phones and GPS units are handy, they aren't always reliable in the backcountry; consider carrying a paper map and compass as a backup and know how to use them.

3. Water (and a way to purify it)

As a guideline, plan for half a liter of water per hour in moderate temperatures/terrain. Carry enough water for your trip and know where and how to treat water while you're out on the trail.

4. Food

Pack calorie-dense foods to help fuel your hike, and carry an extra portion in case you are out longer than expected.

5. Rain Gear and Dry-Fast Layers

The weatherman is not always right. Dress in layers to adjust to changing weather and activity levels. Wear moisture-wicking cloths and carry a warm hat.

6. Safety Items (light, fire, and a whistle)

Have means to start an emergency fire, signal for help, and see the trail and your map in the dark.

7. First Aid Kit

Supplies to treat illness or injury are only as helpful as your knowledge of how to use them. Take a class to gain the skills needed to administer first aid and CPR.

8. Knife or Multi-Tool

With countless uses, a multi-tool can help with gear repair and first aid.

9. Sun Protection

Sunscreen, sunglasses, and sun-protective clothing should be used in every season regardless of temperature or cloud cover.

10. Shelter

Protection from the elements in the event you are injured or stranded is necessary. A lightweight, inexpensive space blanket is a great option.

Find other helpful resources at
AmericanHiking.org/hiking-resources

About the Author

Jamie Siebrase lives in the foothills of Colorado where she explores the state's beautiful terrain with her husband and their three children. When she isn't outside, she's writing feature-length stories for a variety of local media outlets. Her first book is *Hiking with Kids Colorado: 52 Great Hikes for Families*.